Politics and Time

D1222796

Politics and Time

Documenting the Event

Michael J. Shapiro

polity

Copyright © Michael J. Shapiro 2016

The right of Michael J. Shapiro to be identified as Author of this Work has been asserted in accordance with the UK Copyright, Designs and Patents Act 1988.

First published in 2016 by Polity Press

Polity Press
65 Bridge Street
Cambridge CB2 1UR, UK

Polity Press
350 Main Street
Malden, MA 02148, USA

All rights reserved. Except for the quotation of short passages for the purpose of criticism and review, no part of this publication may be reproduced, stored in a retrieval system, or transmitted, in any form or by any means, electronic, mechanical, photocopying, recording or otherwise, without the prior permission of the publisher.

ISBN-13: 978-1-5095-0780-1
ISBN-13: 978-1-5095-0781-8(pb)

A catalogue record for this book is available from the British Library.

Library of Congress Cataloging-in-Publication Data

Names: Shapiro, Michael J., author.
Title: Politics and time : documenting the event / Michael J. Shapiro.
Description: Malden, MA : Polity, 2016. | Includes bibliographical references and index.
Identifiers: LCCN 2015049590 (print) | LCCN 2016015994 (ebook) | ISBN 9781509507801 (hardback) | ISBN 9781509507818 (pbk.) | ISBN 9781509507832 (Mobi) | ISBN 9781509507849 (Epub)
Subjects: LCSH: Political science–Philosophy. | Time–Political aspects. | Disasters–Political aspects.
Classification: LCC JA71 .S425 2016 (print) | LCC JA71 (ebook) | DDC 320.01–dc23
LC record available at http://lccn.loc.gov/2015049590

Typeset in 11 on 13 pt Sabon
by Toppan Best-set Premedia Limited
Printed and bound in the UK by CPI Group (UK) Ltd, Croydon

The publisher has used its best endeavours to ensure that the URLs for external websites referred to in this book are correct and active at the time of going to press. However, the publisher has no responsibility for the websites and can make no guarantee that a site will remain live or that the content is or will remain appropriate.

Every effort has been made to trace all copyright holders, but if any have been inadvertently overlooked the publisher will be pleased to include any necessary credits in any subsequent reprint or edition.

For further information on Polity, visit our website: politybooks.com

Contents

Preface

Three brief commentaries on the event of National Socialism in Germany help me to situate my focus in this investigation of politics and time. The first, by the late sociologist
C. Wright Mills, addresses the responsibilities associated
with the vocation of critical thinking:

> When events move very fast and possible worlds swing
> around them, something happens to the quality of think-
> ing. Some...repeat formulae; some...become reporters.
> To time observations with thought so as to mate a decent
> level of abstraction with crucial happenings is a difficult
> problem. Its solution lies in the *using* of intellectual resi-
> dues of social-history, not jettisoning them except in precise
> confrontation with events.[1]

Mills's observation raises the question of the event-
adequacy of theoretical discourses. To pursue that question, I want to note my accord with answers provided
decades later by Gilles Deleuze and Michel Foucault. When
Deleuze famously insisted that philosophy must be worthy
of the event, he was not simply suggesting that "events
serve to confirm or refute particular theories."[2] He was
advocating a philosophy that privileges critical thinking by
inventing concepts that create the possibility of something
new, by reframing events to allow for new kinds of subjects
and new forms of relationship to emerge.[3] For Deleuze,
such a philosophy must enable an ethics of the event
(a perspective I treat more extensively in chapter 1).

While Deleuze's approach to the relationship between thinking/theorizing and events devolves toward an ethics, Foucault's moves toward a politics of discourse. In one of his earlier discussions of the value of a theoretical discourse (framed as a position on how to interpret the statements in a "discursive formation"), he refers to how to "weigh" the "value" of statements:

> A value that is not defined by their truth, that is not gauged by the presence of a secret content; but which characterized their place, their capacity for circulation and exchange, their possibility for transformation, not only in the economy of discourse, but more generally in the administration of scarce resources ... [a discursive formation in short] appears as an asset – finite, limited, useful ... an asset that is, by nature, the object of a struggle, a political struggle.[4]

In the passage's focus on epistemology, Foucault rejects both representational and hermeneutic approaches to statements, substituting a political pragmatics. What he adds to Mills's observation about the theory–event relationship is a political economy of discourse. Treating statements as assets, he evaluates the discourses in which they function in terms of the resources they differentially deploy, creating spaces for recognition and action by advantaging some subjects of enunciation and disadvantaging others. Similarly, much of my analysis in succeeding chapters offers a politics concerned with the advantages distributed by interpretive practices. As I contrast the mainstream media's with critical artistic genres' interpretations of events, my emphasis is on the way a conceptual framing of events can accord recognition to subjects who are absent in the official discourses that constitute and react to key historical moments.

Crucially, the "subjects" whose recognition to which I refer are not to be regarded as preexisting unities that stand apart from the conceptual frames in which they are allowed to appear. The interpretive practices, resident in a variety of genres, in which subjects are accorded space, participate in fashioning those subjects as historical events. Foucault makes that point evident in his analysis of Edouard Manet's paintings. Manet, he suggests, was the painter most responsible for the emergence of the "modern viewer."[5] In contrast with the world of immobile subjects that had been summoned in prior artistic practices, in Manet's canvases, the spectator becomes "an individual exiled from his certainties regarding his place in the world."[6]

The second commentary on the event of National Socialism I summon is by Primo Levi, a Holocaust survivor (who did not survive his survival). Levi provides an account of a micro event within the larger event of the Holocaust; it's an utterance by a child in his barracks in the Auschwitz *Lager*, where he was a prisoner. The child, Hurbinek, was "the smallest and most harmless among us...the most innocent": "Hurbinek was a nobody, no one knew anything of him, he could not speak and he had no name, that curious name Hurbinek had been given to him by us, perhaps by one of the women who had interpreted with those syllables one of the inarticulate sounds that the baby let out now and again."[7] Levi and his barrack neighbors were attentive to Hurbinek's sounds: "During the night we listened carefully...from Hurbinek's corner there occasionally came a sound, a word...It sounded something like 'mass-klo' or 'matisklo.'" Heeding the child's voiced demand for a presence in the world, Levi grants that presence, allowing "Hurbinek, who fought like a man, to the last breath, to gain entry into the world of men from which a bestial power had excluded him." Specifically, by repeating Hurbinek's word, he lends Hurbinek's existence a duration. His account of the micro event of Hurbinek's utterance renders Hurbinek as a historical subject, playing a political role. Levi's brief discursive gesture constitutes a powerful political pedagogy about the force of a few words. Marking the event of Hurbinek's life and death, he provides an exemplary instance of the ethics and politics of the event. As he sums up his contribution to Hurbinek's presence, Levi writes: "Nothing remains of him: he bears witness through these words of mine."[8]

The third commentary on the event of National Socialism I want to reference is by another Holocaust survivor, the Nobel prizewinning author, Imre Kertész (who survived his survival). In response to an interviewer's question about how the Holocaust has been treated as historical memory in the East and the West, Kertész provides a way to conceive such events: "The Holocaust is an absolute turning point in Europe's history, an event in the light of which will be seen everything that happened before and will happen after."[9] Slavoj Žižek gives us a perspective on the theoretical implications of the way Kertész renders that event: "An event is...the effect that seems to exceed its causes...a change in the way reality appears to us...[perhaps] a shattering transformation of reality itself?"[10]

My investigations of politics and time in this book are focused initially on another reality-shattering event, the dropping of an atomic bomb on Hiroshima, in part because my inspiration for this study is owed to an invitation to contribute to a monograph issue of the journal *Thesis Eleven*, devoted to the seventieth anniversary of the atomic bombing of Hiroshima. Having been recently attuned to a grammar-temporality rendering of that atrocity by Rosalyn Deutsche's excellent book *Hiroshima after Iraq*, I responded to the invitation with an essay entitled "Hiroshima Temporalities" (the prototype for chapter 2, which preserves that title).[11] My opening chapter prepares the way for my analysis of the Hiroshima event in two ways. First and foremost, I respond to the issue of "events" by reviewing and applying the critical philosophical perspectives that shape my analyses and, second, I do a reading of Chris Marker's (semi)-documentary *Level Five* which treats the Battle for Okinawa as an event that helped legitimate the US decision to drop atomic bombs on Hiroshima and Nagasaki.

My analyses throughout the chapters presume that events involve what Claude Romano refers to as "the temporalization of time,"[12] where to refer to temporality rather than mere time registers time as lived experience for particular historically situated subjects. Péter Forgács's documentary work, in which he recovered decades of Hungarian private life by collecting home movies and adding documentary footage (primarily from newsreels to mark the periods in which the home movies are made), is an instance of treating time as lived experience. His approach "marginalizes official history...[in order to have] us understand that time does not unfold through a collective narrative."[13] In effect, Forgács's documentaries substitute the micropolitical aspects of events – the way they bear on lived experience for a variety of individual subjects – for the official national narratives that constitute collective histories.

Heeding Forgács's approach to historical time as a multiplicity of micro events of lived experience, I focus my Hiroshima investigation on a contrast between the United States' official version of the bombing and the experiences of the Japanese target/victims, articulated in a variety of genres and testimonies. I follow that chapter with more temporality-relevant chapters, each of which builds on the problematic that frames what precedes it. Thus because my Hiroshima chapter concludes with a reading of Silva Kolbowski's video *After Hiroshima Mon Amour*, which substitutes a black woman for the French actress Emanuel Riva, thereby reflecting on the ethnic color-coding of events, it is appropriate to follow the Hiroshima chapter with "Hurricane Katrina's Bio-Temporalities" (chapter 3) in which I emphasize the way the hurricane and the policy responses disproportionately victimized black bodies (the African-American population of New Orleans). To treat the inattention to the disproportionate suffering of those bodies, the chapter focuses on Spike Lee's documentary *When the Levies Broke* and David Simon's fictionalized version of Katrina's aftermath in his television series *Treme*, both of which inter-articulate the history of the African-American soundscape with the historical trajectory of Katrina's aftermath.

The Katrina chapter ends with a treatment of what I call the "racial sublime," noting that of late the US media are finally acknowledging that (as I put it with the help of Michael Eric Dyson) "it has becomes evident in a way not previously appreciated by white America, 'the lived experience of race feels like terror for black folk.'"[14] Having appreciated and utilized the concept of the sublime to treat the broader implications of the Katrina event, I enlisted the concept of the sublime to shape parts of chapters 4 and 5, which focus among other things on the sweatshop and weapons sublimes respectively. More generally, the conceptual issues I have needed to think through (rehearsed in the various chapters) are the relationships between temporality and grammar, the fluid boundaries of events, the relationships between official modes of problematization that emerge as "history" versus the lived temporalities of diverse human assemblages; the media and artistic genres within which critical thinking about temporality can be articulated (featured in chapters 1–3); the contentions between the rhythms imposed on bodies by coercive forces (which produce morbidity and hasten death), and the artistic practices that evince the counter-rhythms through which those coercive forces are confronted and resisted (the focus of chapter 4); and the contention between the biographic scripts lent to persons by official agencies (for example, the CIA's bio-anthropologies that select those who are targeted for state murder) and counter-biographies summoned in fictional and documentary texts which challenged the official, assassination-justifying biographies (the focus of chapter 5).

In this brief preface, I want to provide an elaboration of only the first issue, the grammar–temporality relationship, because it shapes not only how I conceive the objects of my investigation but also the grammatical rhythms of my text as I seek to make my analyses "worthy of the event[s]" (to enlist a Deleuzian phrase). My attention to grammar was developed in a prior investigation concerned with the temporality of citizenship.[15] There,

I was especially alerted to the grammar–temporality relationship by Thomas Pynchon's fictional construction of a group discussing a world-shaking, comprehension-challenging (i.e., sublime) event, the decision by the head English astronomer (in 1752) to remove eleven days from the English calendar so that English time could become compatible with other global times (instituted in 1582 by a calendar reform commission under Pope Gregory XIII). As a conversation among patrons in an English pub articulates reactions to the event, one speaker, wondering about "the kind of people who could accept such a change with equanimity," remarks that the astronomer would have to hire:

> A people who lived in a different relation to Time – one that did not, like our own, hold at its heart the terror of Time's passage, far more preferably Indifference to it ... The verbs of their language no more possessing tenses, than their Nouns Case-Ending, for these People remains as disengaged from Subject, object possession, or indeed anything which among Englishmen require a Preposition.[16]

To pick up on the insight provided by Pynchon's character, I want to note that the verb tense that plays a central role in my analyses is the future anterior, the will-have-been, because much of my focus is on the way past events reemerge not only in the present but also enduringly into contingent futures. Specifically, for example, I speculate about how such events as the bombing of Hiroshima and Hurricane Katrina will-have-been after succeeding events give them new political relevance.

The analytics and ethos of my investigation are well captured in a remark by Foucault in his Introduction to the English translation of Georges Canguilhem's *The Normal and the Pathological*: "Error is not eliminated by the muffled force of truth which gradually emerges from the shadow but by a new way of 'speaking true.'"[17] My adaptation of that commitment allocates the "way of speaking true" especially to critically oriented documentary films, whose insights I draw on in each chapter. They are critical in the sense that (to use Deleuze's terms) they are "false narrations," rather than simple chronologies. As a result, they are involved in "shattering systems of judgment"[18] by providing "counter-histories."[19] The documentaries upon which I focus provide challenges in the form of counter-narratives and counter-visions to what Foucault famously calls the "truth weapons" of governments which try to quarantine events within official interpretations, sedimented within (among other places) national museums and archives.

Acknowledgments

While many colleagues, students, and friends have contributed to my thinking – with reactions, insights, and suggested references – I want to single out Sam Opondo who read most of the chapters with amazing discernment and made many helpful suggestions. I also want to acknowledge those who invited me to lecture and/or contribute essays that turned out to be prototypes (or sections) of my chapters: Rune Saugmann Andersen, Garnet Kindervater, Luis Lobo-Guerrero, Mustapha Pasha, Keith Tester, and Juha Vuori.

Almost everything in this book was delivered in lectures and discussions in my courses at the University of Hawaii and at PUC-Rio (the Pontifical Catholic University in Rio de Janeiro). I am grateful to all my students (too numerous to mention) in both places for contributing to the stimulating conversations that affected much of the writing. I want to acknowledge one student in particular, Isabela Carpena, who sat in on one of my courses at PUC-Rio in the summer of 2014 and turned me into a cinematic character. She made a (professionally edited) "Shapiro" biopic in which the rhythms of the montage (mostly film clips and musical interludes interspersed with my commentary) introduce me to a subject/scholar I only vaguely knew. I want also to express my gratitude to my PUC-Rio colleagues for the repeated invitations and support of my teaching of the materials in this book to an attentive and challenging student constituency: Paulo Esteves, Marta Fernandez, Monica Hertz, Joao Nogueira, and Roberto Yamato.

Finally, I want to acknowledge the outstanding support of my acquisition and managing editors, Louise Knight and Nekane Tanaka Galdos, who, along with two anonymous readers, provided valuable insights that found their way into the final draft. A shorter version of chapter 2, "Hiroshima Temporalities," was published in the journal *Thesis Eleven*. I am grateful for their permission to reproduce that material here. And an earlier version of chapter 3, "Hurricane Katrina's Bio-Temporalities" is published in Anna M. Agathangelou and Kyle D. Killian (eds), *Time, Temporality and Violence in International Relations* (Routledge, 2016).

1

Critical Temporalities: Thinking the Event

Introduction: The Battle of Okinawa

"The Battle of Okinawa" is an event that receives relatively little coverage in contemporary reviews of the history of violence, even though its duration and civilian casualty rate looms large in the historical archive of atrocity. It's "old news," and, as Milan Kundera has noted (through one of his fictional characters contemplating the events of brutality that he'd seen covered in recent television news broadcasts), news becomes old very quickly:

> No event remains news over its whole duration, merely for a quite brief span of time, at the very beginning. The dying children of Somalia whom millions of spectators used to watch avidly, aren't they dying anymore? What has become of them? Have they grown fatter or thinner? Does Somalia still exist? And in fact did it ever exist? Could it be only the name of a mirage?[1]

However, as I have suggested elsewhere, "while the momentarily timely images carried by news media may be ephemeral, the genre of the exhibition, which yields an accompanying and enduring catalogue/text, is one in which what becomes effaced as a news event is restored, reflected on, and made publicly available for extended ethical and political negotiation."[2] For example, there is an installation by Alfredo Jaar that references the 1994 massacres in Rwanda. Rather than showing gruesome images of mutilated bodies, Jaar "conceals... photographs of the Rwandan massacre in boxes [see Figure 1.1], after first leading visitors along corridors placing them before a huge screen of light, empty of any image."[3]

Jacques Rancière captures the effect of Jaar's aesthetic strategy: "It is the construction of a sensory arrangement that restores the powers of attention itself."[4] Certainly, diverse media – official government releases, journal, newspaper, television and internet publications, and what is treated by a variety of artistic genres – create the conditions of possibility for what people know about atrocities, starvation, and other forms of adversity all over the planet, and each media genre has a different way of evoking or dulling "powers of attention."

Here, I want to point to another genre, the documentary film, which like the exhibition offers an opportunity for "slow looking" and extended reflection, and, to note one in particular, Chris Marker's "semi-documentary"[5] *Level Five* (1996), which brings back the Battle of Okinawa.

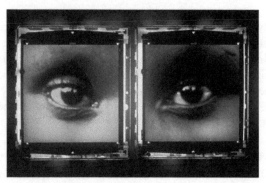

Figure 1.1 The eyes of Gutete Emerita

Combining archival footage with a fictional scenario, the film is narrated by the actress Catherine Belkhodja, who as the character Laura (drawn from Otto Preminger's 1994 eponymous film) sits at a computer console building an interactive video game begun by her deceased lover. The game is aimed at altering the battle. Combining ethnographic and aesthetic subjects – footage of Okinawan informants and victims as the former and "Laura" as the latter (who is continually on-screen, talking to her absent lover) – Marker, a "futuristic ethnologist"[6] as well as a filmmaker/essayist, reframes the way the event will-have-been. Because his way of recreating the past's present and future inspires much of my inquiry throughout this investigation (as well as providing a threshold for chapter 2), I do an extended analysis of the film's complex temporalities at the end of this chapter. However, before turning back to the film, I want to rehearse the conceptualizations through which events can be thought by drawing from both critical philosophical perspectives on temporality and from artistic and cultural texts that implement those perspectives.

Events

To begin illustrating the conceptual interventions I deem necessary for a critical politics of temporality, I return to a subject of an earlier inquiry, a 1996 sports report on a Sunday Giants–Lions NFL game by Mike Freeman in the *New York Times*. Extending the action on the field into a media future, Freeman wrote: "This is an image that might endure in the minds of the Lions for months to come: Giants defensive lineman Ray Agnew, after picking off a pass, rumbling 34 yards for a touchdown, his 285-pound body running so slowly it seemed the feat couldn't be captured on an hour-long highlight show." In my original analysis of the report, I contrasted the value of the touchdown in the game (six points) with that of its potential as a ratings-enhancing "highlight" on a television sportscast.[7] Here, I am revisiting the episode to enhance the "legibility" for what was then the other aspect of my focus, the conceptualization of the layers of temporality needed to capture the episode as a critical political event.[8] Because in my first analysis, I gave inadequate attention to the concept of the event, I turn to that issue first: What is an event?

It should be evident that the constitution of the Ray Agnew event is inseparable from Mike Freeman's dramatic narrative. Rejecting approaches to events that separate them from narratives (as if the "real" of events has a stand-alone facticity that precedes accounts of them) J.-F. Lyotard, using the historian as subject/narrator, writes,

> We habitually pose the following sequence: there is the fact, then the account of the witness, that is to say a narrative activity transforming the fact into a narrative [an intellectual habit that]...poses a theatrical model: outside is the fact, eternal to the theatrical space, on stage the dramatic narrative unfolds; hidden in the wings is the director, the narrator with all [her]/his machinery... The historian is supposed to undo all the machinery and machination to restore the excluded, having beaten down the walls of the theater. But it is obvious that the historian is [herself]/himself only another director, [her]/his narrative another product, [her]/his work another narration.[9]

If we assume, as Lyotard's remarks suggest, that there are no "events" outside of the narratives with which we construct and elaborate them (turning a stream of activity into an event requires interpretive practices that partition continuous time with a lived narrativized temporality), we are able to offer a critical analysis of the way Freeman narrates Ray Agnew's run. What is required in this case is an articulation of philosophical, media technology, and sports histories. Freeman was not a "transparent eyeball,"[10] perceiving a moving body as a pure image, unaffected by where/when he was situated. He occupied a contemporary locus of enunciation, writing as a participant in a modernity that had been shaped by the impact of media technologies on contemporary sports. And we who would make critical sense of the narrative/event are situated in a history of ideas, a critical philosophical trajectory that begins with Immanuel Kant's location of time within subjectivity, runs through Edmund Husserl's concept of time consciousness, proceeds to Martin Heidegger's ontological location of the subject in time, and moves to versions of critically oriented philosophies of history and subjectivity by contemporary post-Kantians – for example those of Walter Benjamin, Michel Foucault, Gilles Deleuze, and Paul Ricoeur, who displace pure consciousness with reactivated possibilities, discursive practices, counter-actualizations, and narratives respectively.

Instead of rehearsing all of the ideational trajectory involved in philosophies of temporality after Kant,[11] I am cutting to what I regard as key revisions of the above-mentioned four thinkers: Benjamin's displacement of a continuum from past to present with episodes of shock, when the past which "carries a temporal index...flashes up at a moment of danger"[12]; Foucault's displacement of temporality from subjective consciousness to discursive practices (privileging especially genres that challenge institutionalized limits of exiting discourses[13]) and to a genealogical version of history; Deleuze's concept of the "pure event" and its various actualizations and counter-actualizations; and Ricoeur's location of time within specific narrative formations (and his privileging of fiction over foundational narratives of rationality, an explicit critique of Hegelian universal history).

Summoning Benjamin first, we can observe a view of historical time that presumes eventual moments derived from a politically acute "mindful remembering," a "seizure in the present of the missed possibilities of happiness in the past."[14] To give that perspective concreteness, we can observe an implementation of Benjamin's view in W. E. B. Du Bois' reflection on the missed possibilities indexed in the post-Civil War reconstruction in the American South. Asking "What is the object of writing the history of the Reconstruction, is it simply to establish the truth, on which Right in the future may be built?"[15] Du Bois goes on to reflect on a missed opportunity. What "flashes up" from the past for him, as he views the racial inequalities, practices of coercion, violence, and exclusion constituted by the "color line" (which etches America's most significant failure to achieve a democracy) is the brief moment when a possibility failed to take hold. He points out that when black entrepreneurs returned to the South, at the beginning of the Reconstruction, it was a time in which "the ranks and file of black labor had a notable leadership of intelligence."[16]

Observing that many white laborers had begun to appreciate the effects of that leadership and that a combined labor force could "bring workers of all colors into a united opposition to the employer,"[17] he saw a possibility of a "democratic development across racial lines,"[18] which never came to fruition. The tragic failure of the Reconstruction was for Du Bois the primary way that the past existed in the present of an America whose oppressive racial-spatial order he both analyzed and lamented. In effect, Du Bois' approach to the political economy of a racially fraught America mimics Benjamin's revision of Kant's philosophical temporality. Du Bois exercised a non-linear, redemptive approach to historical cognition that evokes "the event" by privileging missed possibilities rather than a Kantian *sensus communis*, which is based on a transcendental structure of apprehension. Historical time for Du Bois as for Benjamin is politically attentive. It is not "a linear and homogeneous process whose form remains the same and whose contents, assimilated to persistent forms, are indifferent."[19]

Foucault also departs from the Kantian model of historical cognition.[20] As I have put it (explicating Foucault's later historical method), "Foucault like Kant rejects the iconic thing in itself, but rather than displacing the privileging of the thing with [a phenomenological model of consciousness] a 'productive understanding,' responsible for the shape and temporal extension of phenomena, Foucault substitutes a genealogical practice of historical sensibility."[21] His most explicit approach to the event is articulated in his reflections on Kant's essay on enlightenment (*Aufklarung*) where he shifts the emphasis from the Kantian enlightenment tradition, which enquires into the legitimacy of modes of knowing, to an emphasis on the "connection between mechanisms of coercion and contents of knowledge," an examination of what he calls "eventualization." That expression, which lends a dynamism to the concept of the event, is meant to point to the historically situated "effects of power" generated by the "contents of knowledge."[22] Foucault's approach to the effects of power is in the form of investigations that record the contingencies of power arrangement, making them appear "fragile, temporary [and as mere] events, nothing less than events."[23]

As Foucault pursued his diverse historical investigations, it became evident that the events that occupied his analytic attention involved the emergence of (among other things) new subjects, for example "the criminal," who emerged as a coercion-connected object of knowledge in the middle of the nineteenth century. Whereas prior to that historical moment, "Criminal law knew only two terms, the offense and the penalty,"[24] the mid-nineteenth century witnessed a new subject as an object of knowledge, "the criminal," whose identity began to be interrogated within the disciplinary frames of new knowledge agents, especially psychiatrists, whose knowledge practices were invited into courtroom dramas. As Foucault points out:

> Crime became an important issue for psychiatrists because what was involved was less a field of knowledge to be conquered than a modality of power to be secured and justified. If psychiatry became so important in the nineteenth century, it was not simply because it applied a new

medical rationality to mental or behavioral disorders, it was because it functioned as a sort of public hygiene.[25]

As is the case in his other investigations of subject formation, Foucault locates the event of the criminal's emergence as an object of knowledge in a broader field of events, specifically those associated with the historical development of the biopolitics of population, a shift in governmentalities, beginning in the late eighteenth century, from the problem of maintaining the inviolability of the sovereign to that of managing the social order's collective subject, the "population," which had become "the ultimate end of government, that is the welfare of the population...the increase of its wealth, longevity, health."[26]

Foucault's genealogical sensibility can be enlisted to situate the report on the Giants–Lions game if we observe that what had made Agnew's body into a media body as well as an athletic body is a historical period (an event) that is conceptually captured as what Norbert Elias calls "the sportization of pastimes."[27] There are significant historical moments that precede and contribute to "sportization." One condition of possibility for that event is the historical change from the period in which games had been oriented toward what Johan Huizinga famously called ritualized "play" to commoditized, rule-governed sporting contests, oriented to spectating.[28] An early contribution to that change was the moment in the sixteenth century when the British King James I created sporting Sundays to challenge the power of Puritanism and other religious orders that wanted to preserve non-working days for religious observance. That initiative was followed historically by the development of a different working temporality, the shortening of the working week, which resulted from years of labor militancy that changed the culture of games by creating the time/space for its mutation into sports.[29]

While the impact of gambling has played a crucial role in imposing rules on games/contests that turn play into "sport," which is responsive in part to gamblers' demands for the regularization of the boundaries and processes involved in predicting the possible outcomes of athletic contests, the media, especially the televising of sporting contests, has been even more crucial in the creation of the modern spectator and accordingly the commoditization of games. As two social analysts insist, "The single most dominant influence on the way in which sport is experienced in American society is that of the mass media, particularly television."[30] And of course that "experience" is continuously extended, as fans/spectators purchase sports logo apparel both as fashion statements and as signs of team allegiance.

The change in the sporting body, where the player becomes a media subject who is a spur to media consumption and a shill for commerce as well as a competitor, articulates well with Foucault's genealogical approach to the subject–power relationship. However, my conceptual intervention into the Agnew event thus far leaves open the issue of ethics. While there is doubtless an ethical dimension in Foucault's genealogically oriented history (one of the "domains" of genealogy, he insisted, is "a historical ontology in relation to ethics"[31]), a turn to Deleuzian temporality can help us reflect on the "ethics of the event."

Whereas Foucault evinces the concept of eventualization to point to historical moments in which new individual and collective subjects emerge, aided by new power-invested modalities of enunciation, Deleuze uses the event-relevant concept of "counter-actualization.[32] And whereas Benjamin's politics of temporality looks to the past to articulate a politics of redemption, Deleuze, influenced by Henri Bergson's view of the way the past is sedimented in the present, accepts that temporal imbrication while at the same time privileging the future. For Deleuze, time reaches no reconciliation; the future is always yet to come, driven in a Bergsonian sense by acts of creativity unfolding as part of duration. Deleuze privileges the "instant," articulating "the minimum time" of the instant with "the maximum time" of unlimited duration in order

to "make the instant all the more intense, taut, and instantaneous since it expresses an unlimited future and an
unlimited past, the pure instant grasped at the point at
which it divides itself into the future and past."[33] Without
going into elaborate detail on Deleuze's notion of the pure
event, which operates in a virtuality (containing "the sum
of all possibles")[34] constituting the conditions of possibility for the multiple alternative actualizations of experience,
and for a past that is never closed, I want to focus on the
way he construes ethics as the basis for those moments
that constitute an "ethics of the event."[35]

For Deleuze, ethics is not morality. Whereas traditional
morality is about applying rules for purposes of judgment,
ethics is about embracing uncertainty and becoming eman-
cipated from the habits institutionalized in one's milieu in
order to *think* and thereby be able to imagine a different
world. The look toward the future, which is central to
Deleuze's view of ethics, requires the perpetual " 'ungroun-
ing' of the present,"[36] and among the ways that such an
ungrounding can be effected, according to Deleuze, is
through imitation. To disrupt present ethico-political com-
mitments and practices that are habitual and represent
one mode of actualizing virtual conditions of possibility,
Deleuze suggests that new discourses or practices in various
genres can "counter-actualize" what is fixed by mimicking
a given actualization in order to "double the actualization
[and thus] liberate it for other times."[37]

To illustrate a Deleuzian ethics of repetition with which
one ungrounds the present and actualizes a potential for
different ways of becoming, I turn to aspects of African-
American blues and jazz history, drawing on two all-
too-brief musical lives, those of Jimi Hendrix and John
Coltrane, both of whom enact "semiotic encounters with
the white social order."[38] While many have experienced
the African-American blues-thru-jazz musical trajectory
as mere entertainment, there has been a manifestly political element of the music for much of the African-American
assemblage, which has experienced the music as an

"insurrectional social text,"[39] coding aspects of the past that have received little attention in the mainstream, Euro-American-privileging versions of historical time.

As is well known, much of the blues and jazz tradition speaks to a spatial history associated with the African-American experience – narrativized for example in Duke Ellington's musical rendering of that experience in his epic *Black, Brown and Beige*, which articulates Ellington's "gift for translating visual colors into tone colors"[40] with a commentary on the history of structures of coercive containment and moments of liberating mobility associated with different stages of the black experience in the United States. I analyze Ellington's piece in chapter 3; however, here I want to address and render politically relevant the homology between Deleuze's approach to mimicking and doubling an event (in order to free the present from the fixity of its dominantly received significance) and two musical events, articulated in blues by Hendrix and in jazz by Coltrane.

The Hendrix event is presented by Paul Gilroy, who in effect aligns his observation with a Deleuzian emphasis on futurity as he points to Jimi Hendrix's "unfolding of a cultural revolution that deliberately and self-consciously drew its poetry and soundscape from the future."[41] Referring to Hendrix's debt to and departure from Albert King's "Blues at Sunrise," piece, Gilroy notes Hendrix's "desire to avoid what the previous generation of blues people had done: mournfully to interact with the sunrise of the next day by serenading it, greeting every condemnation to prolonged suffering in the industrialised valley of the dry bones with resignation and defiance" and adds, "The primal scene of Jimi's existential encounter with the prospect of radical autonomy was still dawn, the approved neo-traditional staging." Yet, unlike King from whom he had drawn such compelling inspiration, "Jimi aimed to articulate musical sound that could approximate the power of those first rays in reilluminating and perhaps reenchanting the world."[42]

Similarly, we can exemplify the Deleuzian event with a turn to John Coltrane's jazz versioning of the song "My Favorite Things" from the Rogers and Hammerstein musical *The Sound of Music*. Coltrane had already integrated an aspect of African-American history into his music. His "Alabama" is a composition with powerful somatic resonances that capture the rhythms of Martin Luther King's eulogy at the funeral of two young African-American girls who died in the incident in which "dynamite Bob" blew up a black church in Alabama.[43] In contrast, in Coltrane's versioning of *My Favorite Things*, the political impetus resides more in the *form* of the composition than in its reference. Nevertheless, we have to note at least one aspect of Coltrane's musical reference, the "thing" and how it is valued. Jacques Attali's remarks are pertinent here: "The entrance of music into exchange implicitly presupposes the existence of an intrinsic value in things, external and prior to their exchange. For representation to have a meaning, then, what is represented must be experienced as having an exchangeable and autonomous value, external to the representation and intrinsic to the work."[44] As I have put it elsewhere:

> Were Coltrane's approach to the "things" to which the song refers merely representational, he would simply play the song as originally composed as an affirmation of the value attributed to the "things." What Coltrane does instead is to repeat rather than represent. To the original tune, he adds seven bars in E minor and twenty-three in E major, repeating the melody within different chordal harmonies.[45]

To frame Coltrane's re-inflections of Euro-America's musical actualizations of its self-understandings and his assertion of an African-American shadow world, which has historically practiced its own musical counter-actualizations, we have to recognize the linguistic intelligibility prerequisites to musical intelligibility in general. For that purpose, the appropriate framework derives from Roman Jacobson and Morris Halle's analysis of the "patterning and functioning of language."[46] They point out that the capacity to speak intelligibly operates on an "ascending scale of freedom." One has "zero" freedom with respect to phonemes, for there is a restricted set of possible sounds. However, there is somewhat more freedom for creating combinations – restricted only in terms of the possibilities for coining new words. And, finally, "in the combination of sentences into utterances, the action of compulsory syntactical rules ceases, and the freedom of any individual speaker increases substantially."[47]

Doubtless, Jacobson and Halle were innocent of the creative word games involved in "black talk" – practices of signifying that have existed within what Henry Louis Gates refers to as "the African American discursive forest."[48] And certainly the legacy of African-American signifying practices – a "telling misuse inflicted on English, an abuse which brings the referent more explicitly to light"[49] – is articulated in Coltrane's jazz versioning. However, Coltrane went well beyond mere signifying as he strove to challenge reigning structures of musical intelligibility, seeking to extract as much freedom to mean as the structures of musical language could permit. To put the issue within the Jacobson–Halle frame, focused on the "patterning and functioning of language," whereas the jazz versioning of Thelonious Monk is exercised on the horizontal axis of musical language – by using different pacing, Monk "makes hesitation eloquent"[50] – Coltrane's improvisations play along the vertical axis of musical language by changing chordal harmonies. Coltrane enacts an "articulation of chords with selective pitches or differing accents" in a contrapuntal narrative that recalls the "call and response" or the "doubleness" of "assertion and counter-assertion" associated with practices of "black language games,"[51] effecting a "dissonance," which (as Duke Ellington points out) "is our [the African-American] way of life in America ... We are something apart, yet an integral part."[52]

With his repetitive versioning of a simple show-tune melody, Coltrane stages an encounter between two spatial histories: the settled, self-affirming comfort one takes in a melodic expression of the pleasure of an object of desire, enjoined by an assemblage that takes comfort in knowing who it is, and an unsettled assemblage of people who have had to struggle for a legitimate historical presence and make themselves known through forms of imitation that creatively abuse settled meaning systems. As I've put it, "Desiring to keep the issue of belief and the dominant structures of (musical) intelligibility open, Coltrane evinced a non-closural musical grammar (he reported that he wanted to 'learn how to start in the middle of a sentence and move in both directions at the same time')."[53] He thus entered what Deleuze calls the "theater of repetition" rather than that of representation, where the latter is aimed at deepening rather than destabilizing allegiances:

> The theater of repetition is opposed to the theater of representation...in the theater of repetition we experience pure forces, dynamic lines in space which act without intermediary upon the spirit, and link it directly with nature and history, with a language which speaks before words, with gestures which develop before organized bodies, with masks before faces, with specters and phantoms before characters – the whole apparatus of repetition as a "terrible power."[54]

Ultimately, to appreciate critical challenges to dominant practices of temporality (for example, universalist models of historical time), we have to summon events of encounter that disturb those models and at the same time consider the narrative genres best able to articulate them. Paul Ricoeur's epic investigation of the time–narrative relationship provides the relevant conceptual apparatus for such a consideration. Examining the temporal structures of narrative in historical and fictional discourses, Ricoeur privileges fiction's capacity for rendering temporal multiplicity.

"Fiction," he asserts, "...is a treasure trove of imaginative variations applied to the phenomenology of time and its aporias."[55] Pointing to Marcel Proust's peerless treatment of the embodied sensibility one has of time, Ricoeur refers to "the polarity between time consciousness and the time of the world."[56] And "[t]racing the path from [Virginia Woolf's] *Mrs. Dalloway* to [Thomas Mann's] *The Magic Mountain* to [Proust's] *Remembrance of Things Past*," he points out that "fiction removes the partitions between problems that the *aporetics* of time had carefully separated." Juxtaposing "lived" or "phenomenological" time and "world" or "historical" time, Ricoeur suggests that the latter conceals the former "due to the very fact that it is set within the great chronology of the universe."[57] Jacques Rancière (focusing on painting rather than novels) concurs with Ricoeur's privileging of the multiplicity-capacity of artistic works, noting that their effect is especially evident in museum collections, where many stand side by side: "Artistic ruptures became possible...because the museum offered a multiplication of temporalities of art, allowing for instance Manet to become a painter of modern life by re-painting Velasquez and Titian."[58]

However, the multiplicity that Ricoeur sees in fiction is qualified and restricted by his seeming approval of Alfred Schutz's suggestion that "we share a community of time" because "we are growing old together."[59] That limitation within Ricoeur's insightful abstractions, which confine multiplicity within a single aspect of a shared life narrative, is effectively challenged by the Mexican writer Carlos Fuentes in a report on an event of encounter. Lost while driving with American friends in the Morelos section of Mexico, Fuentes asked a local peasant (*campesino*) the name of the village they were in. Despite the attenuation of "local times" that had by then begun to "collapse once the framework of a global electronic network was established,"[60] that villager remained in a local time. He replied. "That depends, we call the village Santa Maria in times of peace. We call it Zapata in times of war."[61]

Reacting to the remark, Fuentes "ascribes to the old *campesino* a knowledge that 'most people in the West have assiduously ignored since the seventeenth century: that there is more than one time in the world, that there is another time existing alongside, above, underneath the linear calendars of the West."[62] The event of Fuentes's sudden discovery of temporal plurality effectively reproduces a fundamentally Proustian insight, well summarized by Deleuze: "In opposition to the philosophical idea of 'method,' Proust sets the double idea of 'constraint' and of 'chance.' Truth depends on an encounter with something that forces us to think and to seek the truth."[63] That "truth" for Proust is articulated as a semiotics in which every encounter with signs produces two crucial insights: "Time itself (*le Temps*) is plural," and every "passing time...alters beings and annihilates what once was."[64]

The surmise that Fuentes adopts after his Proustian moment is in accord with Ricoeur's privileging of the capacity of fiction to articulate temporal multiplicity. Fuentes goes on to refer to the capacity of his vocation: "The novel," he insists, "is the literary form, that with most complexity, permits us to reappropriate time."[65] And Fuentes has demonstrated the novel's capacity for articulating temporal complexity throughout his writing career. For example, in his last novel, *Destiny and Desire*, a literary intervention into Mexico's narcopolitics, he addresses Mexico's historical time, which he characterizes as a form of state governance that has been about ensuring popular submission to structures of class privilege by managing the illusion that it governs a "democracy" where, more realistically, "The history of Mexico [up to the point where crime replaces the state] is a long process of leaving behind anarchy and dictatorship and reaching a democratic authoritarianism."[66] He contrasts the lived, experiential time of diverse types as his protagonists/aesthetic subjects reflect the biographical time of people with different heredities and class backgrounds and different vocations as they attempt to manage a political reality characterized by Fuentes as "the great

drama of Mexico [in which] crime has replaced the state."[67]
Fuentes's privileging of the novel's capacity for temporal
multiplicity notwithstanding, other artistic genres, especially cinema (whether in the form of the feature films or
documentaries), have a similar capacity. And, as the case of
the Russian director Sergei Eisenstein shows, the development of cinematic montage was influenced by the temporal
play of novels, specifically those of Dickens in Eisenstein's
case: "Dickens," Eisenstein writes, "was the first to bring
factories, machines, and railways into literature...[and his
urbanism] may be found not only in his thematic material,
but also in the head-spinning impressions with which
Dickens sketches the city in the form of a dynamic (montage)
picture."[68]

Certainly, it is Deleuze, who more than any other thinker
has theorized cinema's capacity for illustrating and inter-
articulating temporal layers, mainly in his analysis of the
way the "time-image," a direct rendering of time through
editing, evinces critical, politically relevant thinking.
However, rather than explicating the details of Deleuze's
analysis of the time image, I offer a brief illustration I have
discussed elsewhere, based on Deleuze's suggestion that
"depth of focus shots articulate sheets of time (especially
notable in the films of Orson Welles and Alain Resnais in
which 'sheets of past coexist and confront each other' ")[69]

In his film *Beneath Clouds* (2002), Ivan Sen has his
characters, a Murri (Aboriginal) young man, Vaughan,
and a part-Aboriginal, part-Irish young woman, Lena,
meet while traveling through an Australian landscape. As
I noted in a prior treatment of the film,

> The time images of the landscape shots combine with the
> images of Lena and Vaughan to create a critical exchange
> between the biographical time of the characters and Aus-
> tralian settler time...Sen's writing-through-image editing
> [conveys the] struggles of those who manifest varying
> degrees of aboriginality to accommodate to a place where
> aboriginality has been largely overcoded by the signs of
> Euro-Australian settlement.[70]

While as a narrative the film reaches no dramatic conclusion, the film's landscape and close-up face and body
shots carry the burden of its political thinking. Sen's concatenation of images transcends the plot as his shots and
editing show both the emotionally charged and complex
ethnic mix of Australia by focusing on eyes and the historic
ethnic fault line between Euro and Aboriginal Australians
by cutting to panoramic and deep-focus landscape shots.
The close-ups of eyes, some blue (e.g., belonging to a
mixed, Irish-Aboriginal teenage girl) and some dark brown
(e.g., belonging to a Murri teenage boy), deliver the complexity of Australia's ethnoscape. The cuts from eyes to
landscape shots, some of which show vast expanses devoid
of enterprises, some of which show industrial interventions
in the landscape, and one of which shows a looming
mountain, filtered in a way that spiritualizes it, demon-
strate the multiplicity of ways in which the land is
occupied both experientially and symbolically. That the
landscape is spirtualized by Aborigines is voiced at one
point by Vaughan, who tells Lena, as they walk past a cliff
face, that they are moving past a "sacred site."

Ultimately, Sen mounts a cinematic challenge to the
history of Euro-Australian landscape imagery, especially
the Euro-Australian landscape painting tradition, which is
largely oriented toward showing "the construction of a
new land" in the light of "the ambivalent background of
the Aboriginal presence."[71] Insofar as Aborigines show up
as part of Australia's historical time in Euro-Australian
landscape painting genre, the tendency has been to represent them as peripheral to the work of nation-building –
for example, representing them "at home in the sublime
[and as]...strangers to the world of work, as it is conceived by the settler."[72]

Sen's counter-actualization of the settler narrative does
not privilege a single viewpoint. Shots taken from the viewpoints of the different characters, alternating through cuts
and juxtapositions, with images that often contradict their
expressed viewpoints, show that subjective perception is not

what commands interpretation. And with his depth of focus shots of the landscape and his panning shots that locate his characters and interactions in spatial contexts, Sen lends spatio-temporal expression to his drama, articulating political implications that exceed the particular moments experienced by the bodies moving across the landscape. Ultimately, in Sen's film, the spatio-temporality of Australia exceeds the experiences of immediate sensation to which the characters are meant to react. His Australia is lent temporal depth through the way his rendering the landscape thinks about the history of Australia's inter-ethnic politics.

Documentary cinema has a similar capacity for expressing temporal layering, for it "shares [with]...its fictional counterpart" the editing effects that create a critical political story: "high or low camera angles...close-ups which trade emotional resonance for spatial integrity, the use of telephoto or wide-angle lenses which squeeze or distort space, the use of editing to make time contract, expand or become rhythmic."[73] For example, in Errol Morris's biopic, *The Fog of War: Eleven Lessons from the Life of Robert McNamara* (2003), in which he inter-articulates two narrative threads – the story of McNamara's career and his role in shaping US war policy (as Secretary of Defense) – McNamara believes that his words and gestures control interpretations of his actions. However, with a montage of images, Morris creates a counter-actualization of the events in which McNamara was involved. While McNamara's narrative of events from the Cuban missile crisis through the Vietnam War (and his prior role in the Office of Statistical Control during World War II) emphasizes the danger to the survival of nation-states, Morris's concatenation of images emphasizes civilian casualties in two kinds of image sequence, speeded-up shots of people walking through urban settings and symbolic images in which numbers instead of bombs are dropping on Japanese cities during World War II (as on-screen calculations show how much of the population of counterpart US cities would have been killed). The result of the documentary, which through its

editing and camera angles (McNamara is continually displaced from the center of the screen) is to turn a narrative
of the rationalities used by those managing reasons of state
into a rationality that justifies exterminism, which McNamara tries to dissimulate as a series of edifying historical
lessons. As Morris's film demonstrates, documentaries (like
feature films) achieve their critical effects through time
images that disrupt official versions of historical time.

Where does the viewer fit in such a cinematic treatment
of history? To approach that question, we have to heed the
phenomenological relationship between the temporality of
cinema (both feature films and documentaries) and the
lived time of viewer consciousness. The film-viewing experience is an encounter of tempos and rhythms because
duration is part of consciousness as well as of the material
world; there is a rhythm in both domains, as Henri Bergson
points out. As a result, the meeting of "mind and matter"
constitutes a meeting of durations, however "enormous
[may be the] difference between the rhythm of our own
perceptual duration and the rhythm of the duration of
matter."[74] Thus, for example, while for decades many
viewers have watched Gillo Pontecorvo's politically engaged
The Battle of Algiers (1966) to reflect on the history of the
violence of colonial repression and the persistence of anti-
colonial nationalist movements, members of the US Pentagon, who brought to their viewing a different durational
mentality (focused among other things on the time of intelligence gathering), watched the film during the post-9/11
wars in Iraq and Afghanistan to learn about the value of
torture and stress-inducing forms of interrogation. It is
likely that Pontecorvo's film resisted much of the viewing
orientation of the Pentagon functionaries. Because the
brain-as-screen does more than merely record – it filters
and discards – critically oriented cinema achieves its political effects by restoring what the filtering/excluding process
evacuates. Cinema can disrupt our usual phenomenology
of perception, "removing us from the social divisions of
labor that assign us a role, a function, and a meaning."[75]

Doubtless, as I have noted, the viewers from the Pentagon must have been hard pressed to derive merely functional, task-related instruction from images of "tortures which include electric shock, near drowning, blowtorch burning and upside down hanging" in a film that foregrounds "a situation of curtailed freedom in which...'the riches of the one [French colonials] are built on the poverty of the other [Algerians].'"[76] Other artistic genres, for example literature, also challenge practices of evacuation and inattention, repartitioning the senses of the world that official framings of historical time have shaped. As Deleuze has insisted (in a Bergson-inspired critical play with grammar), "the past is, the present was."[77] As a result, insofar as the past is being continually changed, it is perhaps best captured with another grammatical trope, the future anterior (the will-have-been) which articulates a changing past while providing an opening to a contingent future of possibility. Louis Althusser puts it succinctly: "History is nothing but the permanent revocation of the accomplished fact."[78]

From Literature to Cinema

The revocations of "the accomplished fact" operate differently in different genres, which I want to illustrate with attention to two versions of a story: a chapter, "The Werckmeister Harmonies," in Laszlo Krasznahorkai's novel *The Melancholy of Resistance* (1998); and Béla Tarr's film version of the story, *The Werckmeister Harmonies* (2000) (with a screenplay on which Krasznahorkai collaborated). Krasznahorkai's "Werckmeister Harmonies" chapter begins with a long description, full of diverse temporal references to the activities in a café:

Since Mr Hagelmayer, the proprietor of Pfeffer and Co, Licensed Victuallers of Hid Road...was usually longing for bed by this time and had begun to consult his watch with an ever sterner look on his face ("Eight O'clock,

closing time, gentlemen!"), which meant...that he would
shortly turn down the steadily purring oil-heater in the
corner, switch off the light and, opening the door, usher
his reluctant customers out into the unwelcoming icy wind
beyond – it was no surprise to the happy and grinning
Valuska...to be called upon, even encouraged, to explain
this business of "the erf and the mune", for this is what
he had asked for last night, the night before and goodness
knows how many nights before that, if only to distract the
stubborn attention of the loud if sleepy landlord and allow
for one last all-important spritzer.[79]

The passage presents and places in tension contrasting
temporal frames, each articulating different perspectives:
the proprietary time associated with the opening and
closing hours of the café (a concern of its grumpy proprietor, whose focus is on the rhythms of his sleeping and
waking), the drinking times of the café's habitués (always
seeking to prolong their evening) and the cosmological
time with which the character Janos Valuska is fascinated.
He marvels at the order of the cosmos and is desirous of
explaining its temporal rhythms, which he does by creating
a celestial choreography with the bodies of the café's clientele (choosing one to play the sun, and others to rotate
around each other – the earth body around the sun and,
simultaneously, the moon body around the earth).

In the film version, the first scene is an extended take
that also provides a clash of temporalities, primarily with
images. Like the novel, the film features a contrast between
the domestic rhythms of the café's opening and closing
times and the celestial rhythms associated with eclipses.
The scene begins as Tarr's camera provides an extended
close-up of the café's oven burner (Figure 1.2), which
stands for the materiality of the café's temporal rhythms
(it provides the café's warmth during opening hours).

After the close-up of the oven burner, we see the proprietor, Mr Hagelmayer, dousing the fire with a pitcher of
water in preparation for closing time. The camera then
pulls back to provide a master shot of the café's interior,

Figure 1.2 The café's oven

as its inebriated habitués stagger around. Before long, the choreography of drunken staggering – a typical set of movements in that portion of the life-world – is displaced by the new, imposed choreography by Valuska (Lars Rudolph). Once he has the celestial structure operating (with the sun figure at the center, the earth figure circling him, and the moon figure simultaneously circling the earth figure: Figure 1.3), he announces a celestial event, an eclipse. He describes a dark shadow that grows bigger so that soon only a narrow crescent of the sun can be seen. The scene proceeds slowly. "Like Krasznahorkai's long sentences, Tarr's long take calls for a slow encounter with the material of narrative."[80]

Then the dramatic event unfolds. As he pushes the sun figure downward to represent an eclipse, he says (in the film version):

the air gets suddenly colder. "Can you feel it?" The sky darkens and then all goes dark. The dogs howl, rabbits hunch down, the deer runs in panic…incomprehensible

Figure 1.3 The celestial group

dusk, even the birds too are confused and go to roost, and then complete silence, everything is still…are the hills going to march off, will heaven fall upon us, will the earth open under us? We don't know for a total eclipse has come upon us.[81]

The camera then pulls back from the celestial grouping, with Valuska at the center, as he announces, "But no need to fear; it's not over, for across the sun's glowing sphere, the moon swims away and the sun again bursts forth," at which point he turns and lifts the body of the sun character to an upright position once more and proceeds to recreate the moving celestial choreography, saying that, "the light and warmth again flood the earth," just as the customers can expect that tomorrow they will be experiencing the warmth of the café from the relit oil-burner. They will have gone back to "social time." As Daniel Bensaïd's historical analysis of time suggests, Valuska's intervention is an anachronism in that it brings back "solar time" in a modern period which, since the Renaissance, has seen social time displacing solar time: "From the Renaissance onward, social time supplanted solar time. The reassuring signs of the calendar and the uneven hours of the seasons were erased in indifferently divisible equal hours. Clocks and dials multiplied."[82]

Although the celestial choreography scene is similar in both Werckmeister texts, where Krasznahorkai's novel explores the phenomenological depth of the characters who must cope with both expected and disturbing events, in Tarr's film the camera shots *are* events: "[W]e argue," writes Steven Marchant perspicaciously, "that what is achieved in the *Werckmeister* shot is inseparable from its being achieved in photography. The shot...is poorly understood when conceived as a representation, an act of looking or a window onto events, for the shot itself is an event – a photographic event."[83] In addition to providing the contrast between the temporal rhythms of the café and that of the cosmos, circulating around a stove and sun respectively, the eclipse sets the tone for the rest of the film, which is among other things a long shadow play. Inasmuch as "images are closely related to concepts"[84] (as the film-maker Harun Farocki puts it), what the novel treats with words is often manifested in the film through a series of tonal images, plays of light and dark. Miming the eclipse, dark shadows sweep across lighted areas as vehicles and persons move about – for example, in the scene in which a tractor, pulling a large circus wagon, performs an eclipse as it passes down the street, moving its shadow across illuminated buildings (Figure 1.4).

In Krasznahorkai's and Tarr's "Werckmeister Harmonies," the protagonists are all aesthetic subjects who articulate the action and the thought-worlds involved in creating the violence of much of Hungary's contemporary history and the scars and traumas that remain – rethought in their versions of the story, which challenge the way Hungary's official history has been institutionalized. To conclude this chapter, I turn back to Chris Marker's semi-documentary, which contains ethnographic as well as aesthetic subjects as it ponders another historical scar, etched by the atrocities visited on Okinawa during the World War II Battle of Okinawa. I dwell on that film not only to rehearse the

Figure 1.4 The eclipse on the buildings

significance of the documentary genre for elucidating a politics of temporality (a focus that I elaborate in subsequent chapters) but also because Marker's film provides a threshold for my analysis of the temporalities associated with the bombing of Hiroshima, which closely followed the end of the battle for Okinawa. That exploration (undertaken in chapter 2) is focused on how the bombing of Hiroshima will-have-been after the wars of the present and the future. What will be its predominant facticity and thus its political implications, as continuing large-scale atrocities turn our attention back to that event? The answers to those questions will depend in part on the media technologies through which it is retrieved, as well as how we who recollect it understand ourselves as historical subjects – as Chris Marker's documentary suggests.

Level Five

As Chris Marker weaves "together disparate levels of referentiality and historical narration in his *Level Five*,"[85] he turns the viewer's attention both back to the historical battle for Okinawa and forward to a possible future in which that battle could be altered. His narrator, Catherine

Belkhodja as Laura, begins by reflecting on how strange contemporary technology would look if viewed from the pre-historical past. The film opens with footage of a tracking mouse being moved around on a mouse pad next to a computer as Laura wonders what "mad god" made the technology and imagines a Neanderthal man glimpsing the flashing lights of a modern city at night – "all motion and light" – experiencing the images as unintelligible. The concept of intelligibility then frames Laura's task as she logs on, her hand meeting the hand on screen to yield access to a technologically mediated entry into the Battle of Okinawa. Once her "access is granted," her plan is to "reconstruct the Battle of Okinawa April 1, 1945. The last battle of World War II" in order, she says, to change its "malignant fate." That battle is temporalized through Laura's search, which brings the viewer into the past, back to the present, and toward an imagined future.

Laura is the film's aesthetic subject who guides us through the experiences of the battle and its reconstruction. Inasmuch as her appearance on screen, almost always seated in front of the computer (Figure 1.5), is accompanied by cuts

Figure 1.5 Laura in front of the computer

to characters and bodies that experienced the battle, as well as to contemporary commentators who interpret it from the point of view of the present, she functions as an adjunct ethnographer as well, coordinating both past and present "informants." As a result, the film is both an artistic invention and an excursion into visual anthropology. Marker, the "futuristic ethnologist…a reinventor and reshuffler of realities,"[86] has created a film that combines artistic and ethnographic moments. In James Clifford's terms, Marker achieves a "surrealist moment in ethnography," an "ethnography on the model of collage." Through his cinematic "juxtapositions," coupled with inventions, he is at once a creative artist and an ethnographer.[87] Marker is also a cinematic essayist; he intervenes occasionally – for example, early in the film when his voice figures his role as auto-ethnographic; his voice-over refers to his trip to Japan, where he "shared their [the Japanese's] collective amnesia," their practiced illusion that the battle never happened.

Shortly after that auto-ethnographic moment, Laura, who is again guiding the recreation of the battle, indicates how the technology of a computer search constrains the reality of the objects of investigation. The computer is shown to be "the moral arbiter of her encounter with history."[88] Finding access to the history of the battle problematic and finding herself unable to create a better result from it, she decides to "tease" the computer by using nouns as if they are verbs, typing, successively, dog, sardine, rhododendron, cauliflower, slice-cake, Eiffel Tower, and shoe. In response to each, the computer replies, "I don't know how to dog," "…to sardine," and so on. There are additional technological inhibitions involved in the computer-mediated reconstruction, inasmuch as "the computer is a screen in both senses: it transmits information, but it also has a protective or concealing function."[89] At the outset of her search, to locate Okinawa in the internet archive, Laura types in an O and scrolls down to Okinawa. Subsequently, attempting to recreate the battle, she searches details in the same way – for example typing an F and then

Figure 1.6 Access denied

scrolling down to Formosa (where the US's Ninth Army had assembled before their assault on the island). When she clicks on Formosa, she is denied access (Figure 1.6).

The vagaries of access and denial as Laura selects the terms for her search make it evident that what the Battle of Okinawa is going to be in her game will be a function of the technology with which she attempts to recover it because the computer, like the human mind, is as much an evacuating mechanism as it is a vehicle for inquiry. However, there is yet another significant contingency that will determine what can be found and (re)created. A crucial part of the search is the identity of the temporalizing subject (the creator of the event as a subject of enunciation). Laura is directed to invent a persona for herself. At one point, well into the "pseudo-documentary," an on-screen message says, "Pick your mask." We subsequently see a kaleidoscope of images of Laura wearing various different masks. A voice-over tells us that while in the past individuals had pseudonyms, here they wear circus masks. What do the multiple masking moments that Laura conducts say? Through a staging of encounters between an unstable subject of enunciation – one fashioned as multiple personae bidden to pick both its mask and its informants – Marker fashions an artistic ethnography with a fragile aesthetic subject, who summons informants to recreate a past whose significance can never be exhausted. The Battle of Okinawa's will-have-been will always emerge as a function of the way (technologically) it is summoned and by what kind of subject. Moreover, in contrast with the Kantian subject, for whom time is part of an inner sense, a structure of apprehension, Marker's documentary favors the Bergsonian position. Time is what happens to the subject; it's a main aspect of the way the world resists as it registers its presence.

Inasmuch as the battle resists interpretive capture by any particular subject, *Level Five* is not governed by a solely subject-oriented phenomenology. What Laura is able to discern as she searches the historical archive is not wholly a "function of a rarefied subjective consciousness producing its own apodictic secure contents."[90] The dynamic of temporality that Laura creates (whatever may be the mask she is wearing) is prompted by a "worldly temporalization...the world itself must temporalize *in order for consciousness to temporalize* [italics in original]."[91] Accordingly, there are hints that there are better and worse lenses through which the battle can be recreated. Laura suggests that the better lenses require a degree of detachment (to allow the temporalization of the battle to emerge). At one point, as she is discussing varying levels of engagement with the history of the battle/event, she allocates the ideological orientations through which things are screened – a "Catholic," a "Communist," or "some other kind of bigot" – to "level one." If the interpreter has a sense of humor – being "wittier or funnier" – they are assigned to "level two." Finally, when Laura speculates what "level five" might be, she asks, "Must one die to get to level five?" The seeming suggestion is that the will-have-been of the battle requires interpretation that can end only if and when there is no one left to interpret it. The ultimate detachment is the recognition that the significance of the "event" cannot be exhausted.

Detachment notwithstanding, Marker's film has an ethical force. The essayist, Marker, is also an ethicist. In

addition to providing historical and contemporary footage
as well as testimony from both those who were there and
those who are current interpreters, he supplies an ethos in
the form of quotations from the fifth-century rabbi, Huna
Ben Joshua, to the effect that God always sides with the
"persecuted" (even when a good man persecutes a bad
man). The persecuted are the Okinawans, a peaceful people
who, as commentators and informants note, were sacrificed in a battle that the Japanese command knew they
wouldn't win. They commanded the Okinawans to commit
suicide and kill those (the children and the elderly) who
were incapable of carrying it out, rather than disgrace the
empire by letting the population fall into enemy hands
(150,000 died as a result). As the commentators familiar
with the historical archive point out, the plan was to make
the battle so costly (in terms of casualties) that the Americans would be wary of invading Japan.

The semi-documentary suggests that the "event" of the
battle leads to no conciliation; it is a permanent "scar of
historical time."[92] Marker's aesthetic subject and adjunct
ethnographer, Laura, registers that scar of historical time
on her body. At one point, she refers to time "drilling
into" her; she suffers she says from "time neuralgia," a
"migraine of time." In sum, *Level Five* is cast as a "memory
of the future." Marker's documentary essay provides a
bridge to the bombing of Hiroshima. Toward the end of
the film, a male voice (Marker's?) suggests that the Battle
of Okinawa "made the case for the atom bomb." And
referring to Alain Resnais's famous feature film treatment
of the bombing of Hiroshima, *Hiroshima Mon Amour*,
Laura utters, "Okinawa mon amour." Thus the Battle of
Okinawa, rendered through Marker's film, is an event in
a Deleuzian sense. Its eventfulness is to be understood not
in terms of what caused it but in terms of its effects,
especially how it opens new ways to think the event
and its future consequences, the major one being the
subject matter of chapter 2, which sorts "Hiroshima
temporalities."

2

Hiroshima Temporalities

Introduction: Endings

It is August 1966 and I'm exposed to two media events at roughly the same time. First, several of us leaving a dinner party shortly after midnight decided to take in "the late show" at the Nippon, a Honolulu theater showing Japanese films: a sentimental genre (for example, stories about beloved elementary schoolteachers) in the early evening and a (soft) pornography genre around midnight. That evening, the late show was Hiroshima native Kaneto Shindo's *Lost Sex*, a film featuring as its protagonist 'the Master' (Hideo Kanze), a Noh theater director who had been rendered impotent by the nuclear fallout of the Hiroshima bombing. The film story foregrounds sex, focusing initially on the Master's potency regained as he is lying in a hospital bed while being subject to the hand manipulations of a young nurse (the scene is shown while being narrated to the Master's housekeeper in a flashback at the beginning of the film). Apart from its sex theme, what the story provides is a window into one aspect of the adversities that were an immediate legacy of the bombing, the physical and mental traumas that disrupted intimate relations. The story doesn't end well for the Master. After a failed marriage, when his potency has once again become fugitive, his 37-year-old housekeeper, a war widow, is able briefly to restore his sexual efficacy by staging erotic scenes in which she is involved. But because he misinterprets the stagings (she solicits other seducers to impersonate him), he breaks off the relationship out of jealousy, only to learn after her death that the seduction scenes were staged for his benefit. The film ends with him as a lonely, unloved man, watching the snowfall at his mountain residence.

The second media event had a different kind of ending. It was a showing of military potency, a simulated bombing run staged on the August 6th anniversary of the Hiroshima atomic bombing and shown during a newscast on a local Hawaiian television station. The setting of the broadcast was an open field at a military base on the island of Oahu. While a group of military families were seated in temporary bleachers flanking the field, an air-force bomber performed a flyover and dropped a smoke bomb. As the smoke rose, a voice announced over the temporarily installed loudspeakers: "There's the bomb that ended the war." The people in the bleachers then applauded. For them, as for many participating in US collective memory, the bombing was "the end" of the Hiroshima event.

At a minimum, the different endings I've glossed testify to radically different experiences of the bombing and different practices of historico-cultural memory in Japan and the United States. Since the dropping of the atom bombs on Hiroshima and Nagasaki, the event has been experienced in the United States as distant and thus abstract. In contrast, as is evident for example in Kenzaburo Oe's *Hiroshima Notes* (prepared after several returns to Hiroshima, roughly two decades after the bombing), the event remains emotionally vivid and enduring for those who were on the scene. As Oe puts it (while observing people visiting "the Memorial Cenograph for the Atomic Bomb Victims), "How often have I seen...people standing still and silently in Hiroshima. On that fateful day in 1945, they saw hell unleashed here. Their eyes are deep, dark-ened, fearful."[1] Certainly, it's hard to imagine the legacy of such an overwhelming violence "compressed into a single instant." The temporality of that event was unique and sublime. It was "not experienced as the cumulative result of protracted battles. There was no gradual interval in which to wrestle with the disruptive rhythm of 'conven-tional' war on everyday life." Rather, "the physical force of [the] disaster overwhelmed comprehension by virtue of [its] sheer and sudden magnitude."[2]

Among what is available from the point of view of the Japanese experience of the immediate aftermath of the bombing is a collection of drawings by Hiroshima survi-vors, turned over to an exhibition entitled "Unforgettable Fire," put on by the NHK, the Nippon Hoso Kyokai (Japanese Broadcasting Corporation). They were solicited after "one survivor brought a hand-drawn picture to the NHK's Hiroshima office"[3] in 1975. Among the drawings is one done by a young schoolgirl (Figure 2.1), who describes the scene she saw (and then drew) while headed from school where she was during the blast to her home at 7.30 am the morning after the bombing:

> I passed by Hijiyama. There were few people to be seen in the scorched field. I saw for the first time a pile of burned bodies in a water tank by the entrance to the broadcasting station. Then I was suddenly frightened by the terrible sight on the street 40 to 50 meters from Shukkeien Garden. There was a charred body of a woman standing frozen in a running posture with one leg lifted and her baby tightly clutched in her arm.[4]

As for American practices of comprehension and recol-lection, out of touch with the Japanese experience after Hiroshima, much of the historical emphasis in diverse American media genres (and to a large extent in academic security studies) has been on futuristic imaginings of a nuclear apocalypse. As for the past, the primary public

Figure 2.1 Yasuko Yamagata's drawing from *Unforgettable Fire*

exposure of the Hiroshima bombing in the United States has been a relatively static story: a bombing run as the apex of the US war strategy, glossed in war history books and in a museum display in Washington DC's Aeronautical and Space Museum (part of the Smithsonian complex). There (as in most other locations as one of Oe's interlocutors laments), "the atomic bomb is known better for its immense power [than] ... for the human misery it causes."[5] Thanks to congressional lobbying that prevented displays and text testifying to the bombing's victims, the Smithsonian's version of the episode eschews Japanese experiences and perspectives and is rendered as part of the history of military flight. The display, a celebration of a US war victory, effectively frames the bombing within a discourse that "attributes national security to air power."[6]

Nevertheless, if we heed Walter Benjamin's concept of "temporal plasticity," a form of time "wholly without direction,"[7] which he discerns in a reflection on the poetry of Friedrich Hölderlin, it becomes evident that because of creative acts in some of the more critically oriented artistic genres, the atomic bombing of Hiroshima has been engaged by a "plastic structure of thought,"[8] a mode of thinking that opens events to future interpretive processes. Because the interpretive framing of Hiroshima, especially in a variety of artistic genres, has been ongoing, "Hiroshima" is a never-ending event; it endures as a variety of artistic and cultural texts ponder it, and it continually reasserts itself in the affective lives of those who have confronted its consequences directly – for example Oe, who wrote (after compiling his notes for publication), "the Hiroshima within me does not come to an end with this publication."[9] The subjects of Oe's investigations must also live perpetually with the experience of the bombing. Those survivors exist in what is "an impossible temporality – it has happened; it is always about to occur – and inasmuch as it impinges in every aspect of the subject – defines the subject as a post-traumatic subjectivity."[10]

Other Returns to Hiroshima

Rosalyn Deutsche captures the mobile temporality of the Hiroshima bombing in her *Hiroshima after Iraq*, where she describes artistic representations that in effect activate the implications of Benjamin's concept of plastic temporality by articulating the event of the bombing with a more recent historical episode, the Iraq War. Conceptualizing the critical temporality that derives from the grammatical tense that locates the past in the future – the future anterior or will-have-been – she analyzes the significance of three returns to Hiroshima. Reviewing one of them, she points out that Silvia Kolbowski's video *After Hiroshima Mon Amour* "returns to Hiroshima to confront the legacy of the atomic bombing, linking it to the present invasion and occupation of Iraq."[11] Recasting the Duras–Resnais film *Hiroshima Mon Amour* (1959) with a different temporal pacing and different mode of oral address, and interspersing images from the Iraq War (and other recent events), Kolbowski creates a heterogeneous temporal association of the two wars, giving both the past and the present different interpretive significance.

To appreciate Kolbowski's intervention and creative play with the temporality of *Hiroshima Mon Amour*, we have to revisit the temporal play in the Marguerite Duras–Alain Resnais screenplay (and in Resnais's cinematic realization of the script). One way to construe the film narrative is to see it as "a documentary on Emmanuel Riva [the actress who plays a French woman having a post-bombing affair with a Japanese man (Eiji Okada)]."[12] Her slow rhythmic narration is simultaneously about Hiroshima, about herself, and about the conditions of possibility for coming to reliable terms with one's own experience and with the experience of the bombing.

Briefly, the film opens with two lovers in bed. We see body parts whose morphology is indistinct because they are too close and the scene is too cropped to allow the viewers certainty of what they are seeing. Duras describes the opening:

As the film opens, two pairs of bare shoulders appear little by little. All we see are these shoulders – cut off from the body at the height of the head and hips – in an embrace, and as if drenched with ashes, rain, dew, or sweat, whichever is preferred. The main thing is that we get the feeling that this dew, this perspiration, has been deposited by the atomic "mushroom" as it moves away and evaporates. It should produce a violent, conflicting feeling of freshness and desire.[13]

In contrast with a geopolitical security story in which the bodies of Japanese victims are rendered in an abstract war discourse as "casualties," the film renders bodies in two experiential registers: the bombing's effects on relations of intimacy and the specifics of the bombing's inscription on bodies. Bringing the two registers together – the event time of the devastating bombing and the micro-temporality of the rhythms of intimacy – the lovers at first "seem to be under a rain of ash," and later their skin looks clear and smooth, showing a light film of the sweat of erotic effort. In a few brief cinematic moments their skin therefore registers moments of "both pleasure and pain."[14]

Doubtless *Hiroshima Mon Amour* challenges the various narratives of the Hiroshima bombing that have shaped US collective memory, which usually includes a persistent "visuality of the atom bomb,"[15] rendered as a mushroom cloud. In the absence of images of the specific devastation to bodies and dwellings, that iconic shape serves as a sublime image-reference to US national security. Seen by most as a still picture radically cut off from event time, it is a static image that effaces the process of devastation that occurred on the ground during and after the explosion. Before elaborating the formal and substantive details of the Duras–Resnais film, I want to cut away from its way of inter-articulating temporalities and turn to an account that, like the film, substitutes the drama of unfolding catastrophic experiences for the stasis of the pervasive US renderings of the bombing (for example, those in the Smithsonian and in archival and print media photographs, and the "museumication" of the Japanese renderings in the Peace Museum in Hiroshima's Peace Square).

Mushrooms and Jellyfish

Although the expression "mushroom cloud" is incorporated in a few places in Masuji Ibuse's classic novelistic account of the Hiroshima bombing, *Black Rain*, its narrator/protagonist Shizuma Shigematsu sees it also as a "jellyfish cloud."[16] That imagery is a stunning alert. It bids us recognize that Ibuse's aesthetic subject, who provides a trenchant witnessing of the aftermath of the bombing, is seeing the cloud in real time. The scenes he reports are thus cinematic rather than photographic; the cloud appears as a mass of undulating motion whose color was fading before his eyes. Although he is a fictional character, Ibuse's "Mr Shizuma," who manages fraught familial intimacy issues while collecting and interpreting the scenes of the devastated cityscape, awash in dead, dying, and sick bodies, conveys much of what Ibuse himself learned at the scene of the bombing, where before writing his novel he had collected diaries and interviews with victims and other residents. Effectively mimicking Ibuse's actual experience of the aftermath of the bombing, his Mr Shizuma performs the novel's narrative as his "journal of the bombing," written with a "Chinese brush and ink."[17]

Through Mr Shizuma's narration, Ibuse's *Black Rain* delivers the temporalities of the bombing's aftermath, not only with the dynamics of the visuals (images of the cloud as an undulating jellyfish, of bodies in various stages of morbidity and decrepitude, and of buildings destroyed or in the process of falling apart) but also in the developing discourses with which those victimized and/or in the vicinity of the bombing come to terms with their experience. One of those discourses is about the weapon. Over time, the description of what had been dropped on Hiroshima's residents changed. At first, it is called a "new weapon," then a "new-type bomb," followed by a "high-capacity bomb," and finally, once more information had become available, an "atomic bomb."[18] At the same time, various aspects of the management of everyday life unfold as resources become scarce. Despite a post-bombing state of emergency that requires a rapid restoration of services, bureaucracies continue to function with their usual temporal pacing. For example, in response to the coal shortage brought to the attention of the "control station" by a petition from Mr Shizuma, the lieutenant in charge says, "concerning coal as I have said many times already...we must

hold a conference before we can come to any conclusion…I'm afraid you'll have to wait until we've held our
conference."[19]

More pervasively, the rhythms of everyday life are
shown to be disturbed. The novel treats in great detail the
culinary practices that must be radically altered because of
severe shortages. And the (non-material) aesthetic practices are also compromised. At one point, Mr Shizuma
writes, "Emerging from the main gate of the Clothing
Depot, I'm struck by the desolation of the lotus pond." He
goes on to reminisce about his former daily enjoyment of
the surroundings: "the glossy black sheen of the crows'
plumage in the morning blends well with the green of the
rice plants, and equally well with the rice fields after they
have started to turn yellow."[20] However, most central to
the plot are the traditional processes of courtship, marriage, and human intimacy, which occupy the novel's main
narrative. The primary focus of this dynamic is on Mr
Shizuma's niece, Yasoku, on whom atom-polluted black
rain has fallen, giving her intermittent bouts of radiation
sickness. As rumors of her illness spread, she is unable
to consummate an engagement. Although that narrative
thread is the major way in which the novel treats the disruption of intimacies, there are other impacts addressed as
well. Mr Shizuma notes for example that he has heard two
characters say that "those injured by the bomb, even if
only slightly hurt, had lost all interest in sex."[21]

Ultimately, Ibuse's *Black Rain* "lays the small human
preoccupations and foibles…against the mighty purposes
of the state…against the threat of universal destruction,
he sets a love form and sense of wonder at life in all its
forms."[22] The novel is a life-affirming micropolitics of the
Japanese social world. It explores the destruction and disruption of the vital rhythms of Japanese life that have
resulted from the necropolitics of state antagonisms.
Appalled by that reality, Ibuse's Mr Shizuma makes the
case for a continuing ethical reflection on the Hiroshima
bombing. He writes that he is afflicted by the thought that

what has happened to the inhabitants constitutes a "moral damage" that will persist well into the future, adding, "In olden times, people used to say that in an area badly damaged by war it took a century to repair the moral damage done to the inhabitants."[23]

The Morality of Forms

Mr Shizuma's remark about the moral damage wrought by the bombing of Hiroshima provides for a propitious return to Duras–Resnais's *Hiroshima Mon Amour*. In accord with the focus of Ibuse's *Black Rain* (and Kaneto Shindo's *Lost Sex*) on the bombing's disruption of processes and structures of desire and intimacy, the film creates a transversality between a love story and the material and social destruction of the city. The film's main narrative thread is a love affair between an unnamed French actress from the city of Nevers, referred to as Elle, and an unnamed Japanese architect from Hiroshima referred to as Lui. The film develops a critical disjuncture at the outset as their bodies connect in mutual passion while their conversation is dissensual. The lovers begin their conversation this way:

> *He*: You saw nothing in Hiroshima. Nothing.
> *She*: I saw everything. Everything.

At the same time that the conversation is dissensual, there is a stark disjuncture between what Elle narrates and what the viewer sees. She notes, for example, that by the fifteenth day, a vast profusion of blooming flowers are poking up through the ashes, "unheard of in flowers before then." At that moment, however, what is shown is morbidity rather than vitality; damaged, grotesque bodies are on screen, being treated by medical staff. The musical score also underscores the dissensus. Early on, it has a rapid, frenetic pace, which adds to the tension between Elle's statements of what she sees and what is shown. In contrast, during Lui's rebuttals, his remarks are backed by a contrapuntal, single instrument (seeming to be a wood-wind), which contrasts with the flute and string accompaniment to Elle's insistences.

With such disjunctive juxtapositions and other aspects of film form, *Hiroshima Mon Amour* establishes a temporal trajectory for what *Black Rain*'s Mr Shizuma calls "moral damage." The film literally puts flesh on that expression, animating the process of bodily disintegration. At the same time, it tracks processes of witnessing while producing a diremption between witnessing and knowing. In response to Lui's frequent assertions that she saw nothing, Elle reports the evidence of her eyes: for example, "I saw the hospital, I'm sure of it...how could I not have seen it." However, when stating that she saw what was in the museum in Peace Square "four times," she introduces uncertainty into that witnessing by evoking the concept of lack; referring to how the museum reconstructs the Hiroshima event, she calls it a "reconstruction for lack of anything else."

As Elle's narrative voice proceeds, the film evokes a distrust of fixed images and iconic representations. An epistemology of the gaze must give way to an epistemology of becoming, an articulation of sense memory with a grammatical framing of history that reaches toward an uncertain future. That valuing of becoming operates in the interface between narrative and image. During her remarks about seeing and knowing what is in the museum, there is a tracking shot of a mother and children approaching the museum and further tracking shots that explore the outside and inside of the building. What can we make of those cinematic moments? Jean-Luc Godard's provocative suggestion is that the aesthetic and moral aspects of the film coincide. In response to a query about whether the film is jarring aesthetically or morally, he says, "Tracking shots *are* a question of morality."[24]

Affirming Godard's observation, the film incessantly juxtaposes the memory of the Hiroshima bombing to the movement of bodies involved in war tourism, especially by cutting from tracking shots of the memorial venues in Peace Square to cuts to hands caressing skin. What is therefore contrasted is a fixed institutionalized realization of the bombing (a fetishizing of the event in buildings, posters and glass cases) and a dynamic bodily sense memory, as the two lovers caress each other's skin while at the same time verbally questioning their different loci of enunciation and the experiential trajectories that have brought them together. That they represent two different temporal trajectories – the war experience of Elle, who is shamed in her city of Nevers because of an affair with a German soldier, and of Lui who has resided in Hiroshima but was not near ground zero during the bombing – is subtly represented by the crossing of their two wristwatches on the night stand of the bed where they are exploring each other's bodies (Figure 2.2).

To amplify Godard's observation about the morality of tracking shots, we can heed the way other aspects of the film's form articulate a morality. It is through montage,

Figure 2.2 Elle's and Lui's crossed watches

the cutting back and forth between the scenes of devastation and the lovers (cuts between the instantaneous destruction of bodies and the slow rhythms of intimacy) that the
film makes its primary moral statements, which are about
the disruption of the temporal rhythms of the life-world.
Among the exemplary cuts that speak to one aspect of that
disruption, interventions into ordinary biological time, are
these: At the same time that the lovers are engaged in a
slow caressing of each other's smooth, unblemished skin,
Elle mentions that when the bomb dropped, there resulted
200,000 dead and 80,000 wounded in nine seconds. And
earlier, as the camera tracks the displays in the museum,
there is a long take of glass containers with (what Elle's
voice-over refers to as) "human flesh, suspended, as if still
alive – its agony still fresh." Subsequently, we see "anonymous masses of hair that the women upon waking, would
find had fallen out," followed by the badly burned
flesh of a man's back. The references to both instantaneous
and rapid morbidity are followed by a scene of the
lovers slowly caressing each other's smooth skin. The contrast between the slow indulgence with which healthy
skin is appreciated and the suddenly damaged flesh resulting from the bombing is underscored with a display of
scorched metal, which Elle describes as looking as vulnerable as flesh.

The discursive and imagistic focus on flesh, along with
the foregrounding of an erotic relationship between Elle
and Lui (both of whom are married), effectively lends the
film a counter-Pauline morality. As is well known, Pauline
theology juxtaposes the spirit to the flesh. Denigrating the
flesh, St Paul mentions among other things, "fornication,
impurity, licentiousness...drunkenness, carousing" (Gala-
tians 5: 19–21), anything that involves the "carnal sins,"
which are associated with a sensual enjoyment involving
"the flesh." In contrast, Elle virtually celebrates what she
calls her "dubious morals." In accord with Elle's indulgence in an erotic *jouissance*, the film suggests that enjoyment of the flesh – of the intimate rhythms of bodily

exchange – is what the bombing specifically and the war as a whole have disrupted. In place of the slow, intimate rhythms of life, the war has produced an accelerated decrepitude (in this sense the film animates Ibuse's primary theme in his *Black Rain*).

Ultimately, through both its cinematic form and discursive narration, the film suggests that Hiroshima (in contrast to the way it is rendered in abstract policy discourses and treatises on apocalypse) is an atrocity that took the forms of instantaneous destruction, sudden impairment, and then the accelerated decrepitude of bodies. At one point, Elle provides a brief phenomenology of the war's attack on the body. After looking in a mirror, she wistfully exclaims that she was young once. That observation calls to mind Imre Kertész's fictional character, Georg Koves, a Hungarian Jewish teenage concentration camp survivor, who offers a more prolix account of the phenomenology of the accelerated decrepitude, in this case as it is wrought by a different war (albeit with a Duras-like emphasis on smooth skin). While he is in the Buchenwald *Lager*, Georg says:

> I can safely say there is nothing more painful, nothing more disheartening than to track day after day, to record day after day, yet again how much of one has wasted away. Back home, while paying no great attention to it, I was generally in harmony with my body: I was fond of this bit of machinery, so to say. I recollect reading some exciting novel in our shaded parlor one summer afternoon, the palm of my hand meanwhile caressing with pleasing absentmindedness the golden-downed, pliantly smooth skin of my tautly muscular sunburned thigh. Now that same skin was drooping in loose folds, jaundiced and desiccated.[25]

Along with the destruction and impairment of physical bodies, the film dwells on the ethics of memory, which through Elle's narration is articulated as a primary aspect of the film's morality. She speaks about the importance of not forgetting Hiroshima – as important she says at one point as never forgetting either her former lover, the German soldier in Nevers (here the city name has special resonance), or the current one in Hiroshima (even though that second love attempts to efface the memory of the first). In order cinematically to represent the theme of forgetting in the present and to do it with a Proustian emphasis on sense memory, the film suggests an equivalence between the two objects of forgetting: lovers and historical events. Elle notes that she had been "under the illusion I would never forget Hiroshima," and she laments her forgetting of her first love, the German soldier: "I was unfaithful to you tonight with this stranger. I told our story. It was, you see, a story that could be told. For fourteen years I hadn't found...the taste of an impossible love again since Nevers. Look how I'm forgetting you...Look how I've forgotten you." The ethics of remembering/ forgetting is doubtless an inspiration for Silvia Kolbowski's *After Hiroshima Mon Amour*, which simultaneously counters the forgetting of the bombing's devastation of the Japanese life-world and suggests an equivalence with the Iraq War.

Kolbowski's and Another after

To appreciate the way Kolbowski returns to and grammatically refigures *Hiroshima Mon Amour*, we have to heed the grammatical play in Duras's screenplay. For example, at one point Elle switches to a future tense: "Asphalt will melt; chaos will prevail...an entire city will be lifted off the ground – then will fall back to earth in ashes." And in another part of the screenplay (but not ultimately in the film version), she shifts to the future anterior, as Elle says to Lui, "You will have seen me." No doubt inspired by those passages, Carol Mavor, analyzing the film, plays with the grammar as well. She suggests, "Hiroshima contains the ashes of Proust's memory of future wars,"[26] Kolbowski is similarly inspired, especially by the "you will have seen me" grammar. As Rosalyn Deutsche points out, as she reviews Kolbowski's artistic intervention that summons the Duras–Resnais version of the Hiroshima bombing and rethinks it in the context of the Iraq invasion and occupation, "The word *after* in Kolbowski's title raises the question of time and therefore of history, which is to say of the meaning of past events."[27] In accord with Duras's grammatical imposition through Elle's narration, Kolbowski's "after" is therefore also governed by the future anterior or will-have-been. That grammar is the analytic with which she reinserts Hiroshima in the present and thereby rethinks both events.

Crucially, inasmuch as (like the Duras–Resnais approach) the vehicles for animating the "after" are bodies involved in intimacy and the exercise of sense memory (instead of the geo-strategic concerns and the technological preoccupations that have shaped US collective memory), Kolbowski's video is a critical intervention into the way that cultural memory will be incessantly renegotiated. Deutsche puts her temporal intervention in clear perspective: "Kolbowski's *After Hiroshima Mon Amour* has a kind of flash-forward structure, one that suggests what Hiroshima 'will have been' by substituting a movement forward from Resnais's film to the present for Resnais's movement backward from narrative present to the past."[28]

Heeding the critical political effect of Kolbowski's intervention (to which I return in the conclusion of this chapter), I want to point to another "after" – Hiroshima after 9/11 as its will-have-been is altered in another artistic event, Linda Hattendorf's documentary film *The Cats of Mirikitani* (2006). Hattendorf lived in Lower Manhattan, very near where a homeless street artist, Jimmie Mirikitani, made and occasionally sold his drawings. Passing him frequently and fascinated by his drawings of cats, she decided to do a short film interview with him, with the thought of ultimately creating a documentary of a street artist:

> It was January 2001, and bitterly cold. He was wrapped in so many hats, coats, and blankets that I could barely see his face. Despite the cold, he was proudly exhibiting his artwork under the shelter of a Korean deli. A picture of a cat caught my eye and we struck up a conversation. It was soon apparent that he was not just selling his artwork, but homeless and living on the street. He seemed so old and frail, and yet full of spirit and life. I was curious and concerned – and I like cats. He gave me the drawing, but asked me to take a picture of it for him. I came back the next day with a small video camera. I asked if he could tell me the stories in some of his pictures. And he had many stories to tell! That's how it began.[29]

The "stories to tell" turned out to powerfully inflect an event that took place during Hattendorf's documentary. Born in Sacramento, California and raised in Hiroshima, Jimmie and his family experienced two kinds of war atrocity. Despite being an American citizen, he and his sister, like many Americans of Japanese ancestry, were sent to internment camps. In Jimmie's case, after being held there for three and a half years, he was forced to sign a document renouncing his citizenship and was then held for brief periods in two other places – effectively forced labor camps – before he ended up in New York and on the street, after the man for whom he worked as a domestic servant died. Added to his being victimized with his illegal incarceration, the Hiroshima bombing wiped out much of his family in Japan.

Recording in his drawings the atrocities visited on him and his family, Jimmie was a practicing archivist. His past was part of a hidden vernacular archive articulated in his drawings. Depicted in some of them are the Tule Lake, California, detention site where he was interned, as well as the Hiroshima bombing. His commentary on the Hiroshima bombing and the internment of Japanese Americans achieved public exposure when Hattendorf's documentary allowed him and his work to rise above the threshold of recognition. Once merely located in the street, where his contribution to the Hiroshima archive was part of a shadow world, it exploded onto many screens as Hattendorf's film migrated from diverse film festivals (where it won several prizes) to theater chains, thereby greatly expanding its publicity. In contrast with the Smithsonian's *Enola Gay* exhibition, which sits in a building as the "privileged topology" for archives,[30] Jimmie's archive, prior to the documentary, had been in the street, a place that has often provided spaces of contestation and renegotiation of the meanings of events. His mobile vernacular archive constitutes a political challenge to the sedentary fixity of official archives. As Achille Mbembe points out, traditionally "the term 'archives' refers to a building, a symbol of a public institution," and to "a collection of documents – normally written documents – kept in this building." Accordingly, "the status and power of the archive derives from this entanglement of building and documents."[31] It is the material presence of archive buildings that effects the power-invested identification and consolidation of the diverse documents constituting the archive, which Derrida refers to as its "consignation."[32]

As Hattendorf's documentary proceeded, the location of the Mirikitani counter-archive became perilous. The September 11, 2001 destruction of the World Trade Center's twin towers occurred, and, as a result, the documentary's temporal focus shifted. To save Jimmie from the toxic air in Lower Manhattan's street, Hattendorf took him into her apartment. While the two of them resided together in the apartment (and Hattendorf became an actor in the documentary, often appearing in front of the camera), they watched the television news together, which she edited to select out aspects of the post-9/11 "war on terror." Near the beginning of Jimmie's stay in the apartment, President Bush's first public utterance about the destruction of the twin towers is aired. Referring to the event as "despicable acts of terror," he goes on to say, "America was targeted because we're the brightest beacon for freedom and opportunity in the world." Thereafter, much of what Hattendorf edits in from television news comes from CNN's version of events, which they offer under the rubric of "America's New War."

As the "new war" takes the form of the invasion of Afghanistan, on the domestic front the profiling of alleged domestic subversion enters the news (a voice on the television says, "Under the circumstances a measure of racial profiling is inevitable"). And as the domestic "war on terror" and the invasion of Afghanistan proceeds, Jimmie provides commentaries: "Can't make war, everything ashes," and "Same old story." Meanwhile, Hattendorf supplies her own commentary with a montage of documentary footage. There are historical shots of old notices posted here and there about the demand for Japanese Americans to report to internment centers; there are scenes of attacks on Middle Eastern Americans by vigilantes (for example, a Middle Eastern face is shone behind a store window that is riddled with bullet holes); and, ultimately, Jimmie's commentary, which had been daily etched, is shown as the camera focuses on his two versions of his experience of the war: several drawings of the Tule Lake internment camp where he was incarcerated (and where, Jimmie points out, many died due to sickness) and one of the Hiroshima bombing that wiped out his family and most of his former schoolmates: "Everything ashes – just like moon... killed babies, children, women, and many old people," as Jimmie puts it (Figures 2.3 and 2.4).

To situate the politics of temporality that Jimmie's story discloses, I refer here to the critical temporality that belongs to the capacity of the cinema. As I have put it elsewhere (inspired by Deleuze on the temporality of the cinema genre), in the films of directors like Alain Resnais, "sheets of the past coexist and confront each other"[33] to produce a critical temporal multiplicity that challenges models of unitary time.[34] However, in the case of Hattendorf's film,

Figure 2.3 The Tule Lake

Figure 2.4 Hiroshima bombing

what is delivered goes beyond mere multiplicity. By interconnecting the atrocities experienced by Japanese Americans in the United States and Japanese civilians in Hiroshima with targets of the "war on terror" at home and abroad, the film imposes an equivalence that constitutes its ethico-political statement. The politics of aesthetics that Hattendorf's film articulates is in accord with one that Jacques Rancière has theorized and illustrated in an analysis of Jean-Luc Godard's film *Histoire(s) du Cinéma*. The film, according to Rancière, contains a "clash of heterogeneous elements that provide a common measure." It creates an equivalence between "two captivations,"[35] that of the "German crowds by Nazi ideology" and that of the "film crowds by Hollywood."[36]

By activating its historical equivalence, *The Cats of Mirikitani* effectively shifts the focus from CNN's and other historical narratives that foreground the "missions" of "America's war" (recall President George W. Bush's "mission accomplished" speech on the deck of a US air-craft carrier) to the war's innocent victims. The film dis-places the media's accounts of the temporal rhythms of a war's strategies with a mapping of the temporal rhythms of an exemplary victim's life-worlds (in the United States and Japan). And the temporal rhythms of Hattendorf's documentary (its articulation of documentary time) illumi-nate the personal and historical times that constituted Jimmie Mirikitani's exemplary experience, while at the same time producing a politics of *jetzeit*, or "now time," (which in Walter Benjamin's sense incorporates the past into the way the present can be experienced).[37]

A New Kind of War and Another "New Weapon"

When Linda Hattendorf's film had the events after 9/11 summon Hiroshima, the Japanese internment, and the life of Jimmie Mirikitani, it turned a story about a street artist into a critical analysis of the contemporary "war on terror." What can be said about the way the emergence of "now time" (how we can have the past in the present since her documentary) bears on the way we can recover Hiroshima's significance? There's a strong hint in a recent observation about contemporary history: "We have unprece-dented electronic surveillance...[and] as with war pho-tography, the technology that testifies coevolves with, and is set alongside the technology that kills."[38] We can go further than suggesting a mere coevolution of the technologies of recording and killing. In the case of the atomic bomb dropped on Hiroshima, there was an almost instantaneous recording of some of the bodies and objects obliterated. The bomb itself was a photographic technology as well as a weapon. Because the radiation from the bomb spread out horizontally in straight lines, the objects in its path absorbed some of the energy. As a result, anything behind those objects – e.g., walls – ended up being either lighter or darker where the objects had blocked the radiation as they were being obliterated. Thus in various places some of the people of Hiroshima and some of their objects absorbed the bomb's thermal energy, leaving shadows on the walls behind them. John Hersey famously supplied and creatively figured specifics: for example, "a painter on a ladder was monumentalized in a kind of bas-relief on the stone façade of a bank building on which he was working, in the act of dipping his brush into his paint can."[39]

Ironically, while the military gaze involved in planning the bombing articulated a distancing anthropological discourse – a macropolitical view of a collectivity known as the Japanese "population" – the technological realization of that gaze, the bomb itself, provided a different more finely tuned ethnographic gaze. It created a micropolitical view of the consequences. What and how do contemporary weapons, the relays of the current military gaze, see? Of late, that question has evoked comparisons between the Hiroshima bombing and contemporary drone warfare.[40]

The drone is a new kind of weapon for a new kind of war, "a war that [according to former President George W. Bush] requires us to be on an international manhunt."[41] Breaking with conventional warfare, instead of a war involving battlefields and an encounter of two armed opponents, the manhunt "is more like a vast campaign of extrajudicial executions."[42] From the perspective of US official policy, the drone contrasts markedly with the Hiroshima bombing and other bombing events that killed thousands of civilians. It is represented as a weapon that singles out enemies and avoids killing civilians. And along with official apologists (in the White House, the Pentagon, and the CIA), the weapon as a realization of the contemporary military gaze has "certain professors of moral philosophy recycled as military consultants" providing a moral epistemology to assure us that the "weapons are *ethical in themselves*,"[43] rather than being a source of what Ibuse's Mr Shizuma called "moral damage."

The remarks of "moral philosophers" on the conditions of possibility for ethical weapons convey a recognition that the military gaze is relayed through the weapons themselves – from rifles with scopes, through armored vehicles, to drones. Under the rubric of "what does a weapon see?" I have suggested elsewhere that in the case of the current weapons *dispositif* (the human–weapons assemblages and their supervising agencies that program enmities, deciding what kinds of subject get targeted), the likelihood of a neglect of the military rules of engagement designed to protect non-combatants increases.[44] In the case of drones, the "pilots" are dealing with a more traumatic scopic field than was the case of the pilot of the *Enola Gay*. While the latter was too distant to observe the specific human consequences of dropping his bomb, drone operators, looking through their weapon, see their human targets (often monitoring them for days and becoming familiar with their social and familial habitus) and have to fire on the basis of deliberations in which they don't get to participate (an issue I treat more elaborately in chapter 5). Who decides on targeting, and what are the criteria that articulate the military gaze through the weaponized drones? Although President Obama has recently tried to shift the targeting decisions to the Pentagon, it remains the case that the criteria usually come from the CIA's security-oriented anthropology. Initially, known persons were selected for targeting by a decision-making group that often included the president and his staff. However, since then, under the direction of the CIA, the warrants for killing have turned from "personality" targeting to "signature" targeting, where the latter strikes are against "men believed to be militants associated with terrorist groups, but whose identities aren't always known."[45] Moreover, the "cultural knowledge" upon which the CIA has been relying has been contributed by a war-friendly social science. The cultural aspect of the war zone, designated with the abstract, distancing expression, "human terrain system," is mapped with the assistance of recruited "knowledge agents" at meetings of the American Anthropological Association.[46]

While official spokespersons, from the president on down, have utilized what Michel Foucault calls a "truth weapon," asserting that it is very rare for anyone other than actual enemy combatants to get killed, doubtless, as Foucault points out, "given that the relationship of dominance works to their advantage, it is certainly not in their [the government's] interest to call any of this into question."[47] And systematic ethnographic work has called "this" into question. A joint Stanford–NYU investigation of the use of drones in Pakistan concluded that, while in the United States the dominant narrative about their use is of a surgically precise and effective tool that avoids killing innocents by enabling "targeted killing of terrorists with minimal downsides or collateral impacts," what they found was an alarming level of atrocity visited on innocent civilians (even though they underreport the deaths of non-combatants): "From June 2004 through mid-September 2012, available data indicate that drone strikes killed 2,562–3,325 people in Pakistan, of whom 474–881 were civilians, including 176 children."[48] Despite official denials, a similar pattern has been discovered in Yemen. For example, "A drone attacked a wedding procession [the second time a drone hit a wedding party] in al Bayda province, killing up to 12 reported civilians." After the organization Human Rights Watch "raised concerns about multiple civilian deaths…, [t]he US has said it has investigated the claims but has found no evidence of civilian casualties. Yet earlier [that] month, *New York Times* reporter Mark Mazzetti, author of a book on drones, wrote that JSOC had been barred from carrying out drone strikes in the country because of 'botched' strikes."[49]

Under such circumstances, it is not surprising, as I've noted, that critical responses to the US drone strategy evoke comparisons with the atomic bombing of civilians in Hiroshima. After the bomb struck Hiroshima, killing mostly civilians, President Truman added a "truth weapon" the next day, stating, "[a] military base had been selected ... 'because we wished in the first attack to avoid, as much as possible, the killing of civilians.' "[50] However, in addition to its evocation in connection with the drone killings of civilians, the will-have-been of Hiroshima is tied to another aspect of US military strategy: the use of depleted uranium on the tips of bullets during the Iraq War so they were able to pierce armored vehicles. As one analyst summarizes the history of "dirty weapons," by 2007 there had been "61 years of uranium wars,"[51] and another suggests that the use of radioactive ammunition in the Middle East will likely have claimed more lives than the atomic bombing of Hiroshima and Nagasaki.[52]

Conclusion: Media, the Ethics of Attention, and Another Hiroshima

As Ibuse's *Black Rain* and other commentaries have made evident, apart from Hiroshima's continual return as it is evoked in comparison with later atrocities, the effects of the bombing were both instantaneous and slow: killing "about 100,000 (instantly)...95,000 of them civilians ...another 100,000, most of those civilians [who experienced]...drawn-out deaths from the effects of radiation."[53] And many have died since over an extended period through mortal injuries and radiation sickness. The depleted uranium left in the Iraqi environment is a legacy that is shared with a host of other forms of what Rob Nixon refers to as "slow violence."[54] Nixon's analysis is focused on the gradual forms of deadly attrition that receive either no or very brief coverage in the mainstream media – for example, the environmental degradation caused by unregulated capitalism, starvation owed to both structures of inequality and violent conflicts that destroy food sources, and the lethal zones left with toxicities, mines and other unexploded military ordinance in the aftermath of wars.

To situate the media practices that neglect or treat perfunctorily this form of violence, I turn again to the passage in Milan Kundera's novel *Slowness* (which I quoted in chapter 1):

> No event remains news over its whole duration, merely for a quite brief span of time, at the very beginning. The dying children of Somalia whom millions of spectators used to watch avidly, aren't they dying anymore? What has become of them? Have they grown fatter or thinner? Does Somalia still exist? And in fact did it ever exist? Could it be only the name of a mirage?[55]

I want also to return to cinema, which is not only (as I have suggested) a genre best suited to provide critical temporal associations but also is in its present historical moment another source of slow looking. For example, as Victor Burgin has pointed out, whereas once the recovery of instances from a remembered film was possible only if the film returned to a theater near you, the new technologies of video reproduction and streaming make it possible now to recover sequence images that interconnect remembered fragments from former viewing experiences in order to explore and create a critical perspective. Enabled by the new temporality of film viewing to analyze the film–memory relationship, Burgin gives us an example of his own experience in which there are sequences from two films. In the first, a woman climbs a path toward the camera and the camera adopts a variety of locations to position her in a landscape (from Tsai Ming-Liang's *Vive L'Amour*, 1994). In the second, there's a long shot of a woman entering the frame, and thereafter, as in the first film Burgin recalls, the camera positions her in the landscape from various locations (Michael Powell's and Emeric Pressburger's film

A Canterbury Tale, 1944). Because the first reminded him
of the second, Burgin was able to replay them in order to
gauge the significance of the way they constitute an antith-
esis: "town and country, old world and new, East and
West."[56] In effect, Burgin explicates the temporal structure
of a contemporary media situation that has enabled much
of my analysis of Hiroshima temporalities. However, in
addition to identifying the relevant temporalities, my
concern, expressed in chapter 1, is with the genres through
which victims of atrocity can be allowed to become part
of public history. For that purpose, I pointed to installations, referring specifically to Alfredo Jaar's approach to
the 1994 massacres in Rwanda.

Here, I want to point to another, which is treated by Jill
Bennett in her analysis of "empathic" forms of vision –
sculptural assemblages by Doris Salcedo, who (like Jaar),
rather than making direct images of people suffering,
creates images that testify to their disappearance, for
example her "Widowed House," which is represented by
"partially dismantled furniture...dispersed around the
gallery space."[57] As these exhibitions get our attention,
they evoke our obligation to recognize "the ethical weight
of others,"[58] whose fates tend to fade rapidly from public
consciousness. Such installations, which reframe the past
by bringing it into the present and opening it to a perpetual
future, show us that (as Jon Kertzer lyrically puts it), "the
temporality of justice is not linear but symphonic...both
retrospective and prospective"; it's an "elegant temporality
[that is] also redemptive; if the past cannot literally be
changed, it can imaginatively be reclaimed for the benefit
of society."[59]

With the redemptive aspect of such a justice in mind, I
want to acknowledge once more the attention-summoning
approach to Hiroshima afforded by Silvia Kolbowski's
video installation, *After Hiroshima Mon Amour*, because
it points not only to Hiroshima as memory and as enduring present and future but also because it helps me to
introduce chapter 3, which treats the "event" of Hurricane

Katrina. Kolbowski's 22-minute installation redoes the film as a video installation and photographic exhibition, which reconstitutes the film as a trauma that migrates into the present. The video begins very much like the Duras–Resnais screenplay with a close-up sequence of bodies, which in this case are ambiguously involved either in an erotic encounter or in a death scene. That scene is quickly interrupted by a night vision scene showing members of the US military, wielding automatic weapons, while intimidating Iraqis. As other scenes are inter-articulated with a miming of the Duras–Resnais film (displaced on different ethnic bodies), the theme that emerges is the official US lack of guilt over its indifference to human suffering in Hiroshima and in subsequent events, notably the Iraq War and Hurricane Katrina (which is sometimes referred to as "our Hiroshima"). Kolbowski seals the connection between Hiroshima and Katrina with video clips of the aftermath of Hurricane Katrina (taken from news

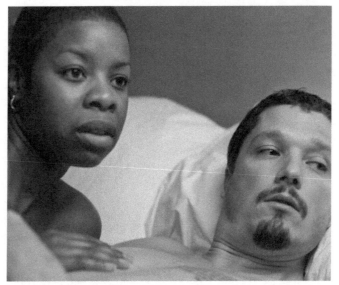

Figure 2.5 Kolbowski's lovers

clips of the devastated city) and with a more subtle reference to both Iraq and Katrina. Recognizing that the Katrina
event disproportionately victimized black bodies, the erotic
scene that Kolbowski invents to mime the Duras–Resnais
version of lovers in *Hiroshima Mon Amour* is between a
Middle Eastern man and a black woman (Figure 2.5).
In chapter 3, on "Hurricane Katrina's Bio-Temporalities,"
the consequences of the event for black bodies are a
primary focus.

3

Hurricane Katrina
Bio-Temporalities

The Discourses of Environmental Disaster

Decades ago, I was struck by the discursive space allocated
in a report in the December 17, 1984 issue of *Time Magazine* on thousands of deaths from a toxic chemical release
at Union Carbide's plant in Bhopal, India. The cover
image, which displayed the bodies of the dead and dying,
was located under a headline that read "Environment."
The implication of that editorial decision, which bids the
reader to flip past the sections on politics in order to find
the report in the environment section of the magazine, was
that the Bhopal incident should be understood as a pollu-
tion accident. Reacting to *Time Magazine*'s framing of the
event, I wrote:

> One can speak usefully here of a kind of ideological script-
> ing of the allocation of danger around the globe. Within
> this scripting, controlled by the dominant modes of repre-
> senting problems of foreign policy and international poli-
> tics, events involving the use of weapons against foreign
> nations on their soil get recruited into the foreign policy
> discursive space, while killing them with pesticide chemi-
> cals does not.[1]

Years later, after Hurricane Katrina hit New Orleans, creating a water surge that inundated 80 percent of the city, I was moved to think again about the Bhopal incident and to consider more generally how the news media create the events that are constituted as "disasters," as they focus on the immediacies of suffering and mortality and allocate responsibility. Typically, while the sudden violence of armed attacks tends to be located in the discursive space of politics, the evocation of a political vocabulary tends to be missing in the case of industrial "accidents" and other events that poison environments, and in the long-term conditions (the "slow violence") that make them possible – what Rob Nixon (as noted in chapter 2) refers to as the gradual forms of deadly attrition from the environmental degradation caused by unregulated capitalism, starvation owed to structures of inequality, violent conflicts that destroy food sources, and the lethal zones left with toxicities, mines, and other unexploded military ordinance in the aftermath of wars.[2]

As a result of the temporal rhythms of news media in the aftermath of episodes of death and suffering, the Bhopal event (however framed) disappeared from the news shortly after the immediate effects were recorded. Nevertheless, "Bhopal" occasionally returns. In May 2004, twenty years after the toxic gas leak, *The Christian Science Monitor* reported that in response to "new environmental studies," the Indian government is preparing to hold Union Carbide responsible for polluted groundwater that is "affecting a new generation of Bhopal citizens."[3] Testifying to Union Carbide's continuing avoidance of responsibility, in December 4, 2004, an article appeared in the *Taipei Times*, reporting, "Two decades after the world's worst-ever industrial accident, many of those who survived injury are still waiting for their compensation."[4] Bhopal was again in the news on the thirtieth anniversary of the event (December 3, 2014). Among the media's focus was the corporate world's ability to thwart compensation claims, while birth defects proliferate as a result of the still-polluted soil and water supply in the area of the toxic gas release:

> The people who suffer are successive generations, almost all poor, whose ill health now affects babies and young children of parents who may not have even been born in 1984. Recently, the Chingari Trust, which deals with handicapped children, staged a play and candlelight vigil in Bhopal's old city. They have 700 children registered with autism, behavioral problems, sensory disorders and developmental delays, some not able to utter any kind of vocal sound.[5]

The posture of Union Carbide (now Dow Chemical) toward the victims of its outsourcing of dangerous work is typical of large US corporations. For example, *The New York Times* reported on November 23, 2013, "One year after the Tazreen factory fire in Bangladesh [in which more than 1,200 workers died]...neither Walmart, Sears, Children's Place nor any of the other American companies that were selling goods produced at Tazreen...have agreed to contribute to the [compensation] efforts."[6] Incidents like the one in Bhopal reveal complex relations among governments and commercial enterprises, located within a "policy dynamic that links strong and weak states...[and renders invisible the] cartography of occupational danger."[7] The dominant cartography achieving public attention is geopolitical/security oriented. The precarious lives of those in unsafe occupations belong to what the novelist Michel Houellebecq refers to as a different map: "free-market economics redrew the geography of the world in terms of the expectations of the clientele, whether the latter moved to indulge in tourism or to earn a living. The flat isometric surface of the map was substituted by an abnormal topography where Shannon was closer to Katowice than to Brussels, to Fuerteventura than to Madrid."[8]

That commercial cartography has been no more sensitive to precarious lives than the security-oriented version

is in evidence in *The Pentagon's New Map*, which, abandoning the former Cold War geopolitical cartography,
allocates friends versus enemies on the basis of business-
and trade-friendly relationships with US corporations.[9] A
discourse on environmental accidents, in which humans
face the vagaries of the elements (fires, water surges, chemical spills, etc.), tends to trump the discourses of the political economy of inequality and the structures of domination
and control. Those discourses, within which a different
mode of responsibility would be enjoined, fail to achieve
adequate enough traction to either protect or adequately
compensate victims. If one takes a perspective that extends
the temporality of vulnerability beyond the occurrence of
so-called environmental accidents, the very concept of the
accident has to be displaced by a thematization of precarity. As Neil Smith puts it, "there is no such thing as a
natural disaster. In every phase and aspect of a disaster –
causes, vulnerability, preparedness, results and response,
and reconstruction – the contours of disaster and the difference between who lives and who dies is to a greater or
lesser extent a social calculus. Hurricane Katrina provides
the most startling confirmation of that axiom." Smith suggests that we should "put social science to work as a
counterweight to official attempts to relegate Katrina
to the historical dustbin of inevitable 'natural' disasters."
In what follows, the "counterweights" I put to work
come more from popular culture than from social science.
They nevertheless support Smith's emphasis on differential
modes of "vulnerability." As he notes:

> Put bluntly, in many climates rich people tend to take the
> higher land leaving to the poor and working class land
> more vulnerable to flooding and environmental pestilence.
> [Moreover]...In New Orleans...topographic gradients
> doubled as class and race gradients, and as the Katrina
> evacuation so tragically demonstrated, the better off had
> cars to get out, credit cards and bank accounts for emer-
> gency hotels and supplies, their immediate families likely
> had resources to support their evacuation, and the wealth-
> ier also had the insurance policies for rebuilding.[10]

Early Katrina

The long-term political economy in which precarious lives are shaped was not part of the public discourse shortly after Hurricane Katrina hit New Orleans (at its peak on August 28, 2005). Among the first frames the media evoked was that of disaster insurance. A *New York Times* report estimated the insurance costs: "Insurance companies said yesterday that damage from Hurricane Katrina could top $9 billion, making it one of the costliest storms on record. While the extent of the damages will not be known for days, estimates yesterday from insurers ranged from $9 billion to $16 billion – down from $15 billion to $30 billion on Sunday."[11] Once the levees were breached and much of the city, especially the Ninth Ward, was under water, another aspect of economy was evoked. Two reporters in the *New York Times* offered a longer temporal trajectory, suggesting that a lust for profits by entrepreneurs led to a willingness to develop enterprises in a precarious landscape: "Although early travelers realized the irrationality of building a port on shifting mud in an area regularly ravaged by storms and disease, the opportunities to make money overrode all objections." And there was an acceptance of an inadequate approach to flood control:

> The Gulf Coast has always been vulnerable to coastal storms, but over the years people have made things worse, particularly in Louisiana, where Hurricane Katrina struck yesterday [and] people learned too late, the landscape of South Louisiana depends on floods: it is made of loose Mississippi River silt, and the ground subsides as this silt consolidates. Only regular floods of muddy water can replenish the sediment and keep the landscape above water.[12]

However, once the enormity of the devastation became evident, the news reports eschewed such long-term thematization and instead began rehearsing a racialized angle of vision that has considerable historical depth and reinforcement in a wide variety of media genres. Evoking a frame for that history, Robert Crooks suggests that the violence that characterized the United States' western frontier during the nineteenth century has been transformed from a mobile western boundary, as Euro-Americans vanquished Native-American nations, into a "relatively fixed partitioning of urban space...a racial frontier."[13] He adds that, in the case of the urban (racial) frontier, there was a refocusing of the frontier ideology – a form of "ideological work" – which is in transformation to the urban setting, involved a morphing of frontiers from the west to urban America, and resulted in a "partitioning," which continued to "map cultural and racial divisions." In the case of the western frontier, a mobile geography pitted Euro-Americans against a racialized, nomadic Native America, while in the urban case the geographical frontier "now denoted relatively fixed lines of defense for the purity and order of European culture [so that they associated] black urban communities with the criminal side of the urban frontier," an association depicted and critiqued in the crime novels of Chester Himes and Walter Mosley,[14] but persisting nevertheless in the profiling of (and violence against) African Americans by many urban police departments.

That "ideological work," which still constitutes the material geographies and imaginaries of the racial-spatial orders of major US cities, was articulated by the news media in the aftermath of Katrina. Abandoning its initial coverage of Katrina's "devastating impacts," the news media turned to a frame that emphasizes "civil unrest," which they attributed disproportionately to young black males.[15] Reacting to that aspect of the coverage, rapper Kanye West said,

> I hate the way they portray us in the media. If you see a black family, it says they're looting. See a white family, it says they're looking for food...We already realize a lot of people that could help are at war right now, fighting another way, and they [the news media] have given them permission to go down and shoot us.[16]

In a less passionate register, media researchers reached a similar conclusion. Distinguishing "episodic" from "thematic" news coverage, they noted, "The national coverage moved from one looting event to the other or from one rooftop rescue to the other, without context...instead of presenting 'thematic' treatments of the region's poor."[17] However, the media's abstractions pale in comparison with the testimonies of African Americans bearing witness to the way New Orleans' racial order affected their experience in the aftermath of Katrina. For example, Emma Dixon reports seeing "painted signs warning that looters would be shot [and being] warned by a white neighbor not to move around too much lest I be taken as a looter." Locating the aftermath of Katrina in the context of an "institutionalized racism that began centuries ago," Dixon states:

> The *unnatural* [my emphasis] disaster of racism swept away the cars with which poor black people could have escaped Katrina. Almost a third of residents of the flooded neighborhoods did not own the cars on which the evacuation plan relied. If the promise to the freed slaves of 40 acres and a mule had been kept, then six generations later, their descendants would own more assets, and the mule would now be a Buick.[18]

Ultimately, although "for most Americans, the horrors of Katrina have devolved into nothing more than a sad but distant memory"[19] "with the pain of Katrina, at least for a brief moment in time, came a great awakening to the implications of race and class disadvantage in America and what that really means in times of crisis. The shocking images of primarily black faces stranded, tired and hungry..."[20] Popular culture texts have extended that moment, evoking the past of America's racial order as they contemplate what Katrina reveals about the persistence of a racial divide. In this regard, I want to call particular attention to a post-Katrina installation at New York's Metropolitan Museum in 2006 by Kara Walker. In her

Figure 3.1 Walker image

After the Deluge (inspired by Katrina), she contemplates the relationship between water and the historical black experience in America. Riffing on J. M. W. Turner's canvas *Slavers Throwing Overboard the Dead and Dying* and Winslow Homer's treatments of nineteenth-century black life in America, she sees Katrina as an occasion for musing about historical oppression in the past, having it "flash up in the moment of danger" in the present. "Known for parlaying the genteel 18th-century art of cut-paper silhouettes into scathing, racially charged installations,"[21] she displayed images on a wall – for example a silhouette of a leisured white plantation couple, juxtaposed with a little black girl, looking at a drowned slave (Figure 3.1). In what follows, I turn to other cultural texts – film and television documentaries – that also extend the Katrina event.

Later Temporalities: Katrina in Popular Culture Genres

When the levees broke

Director Spike Lee's documentary *When the Levees Broke: A Requiem in Four Parts* (2006) effectively counter-actualizes the way the news media racialized Katrina's aftermath and had "rendered the city 'foreign' in relation to the rest of the US,"[22] bidding to alter the future anterior of the Katrina event (how it will-have-been). And it also provides a counter-narrative to cinematic treatments – for example, Greg MacGillivray's documentary *Hurricane on the Bayou* (2006), which "renders invisible...the issue of race."[23] The window that Lee's film provides into the disproportionate suffering of New Orleans' African-American population references an event that has a long historical trajectory. To treat part of that legacy (neglecting some of the in-migration that filled in the city's ethnoscape), the post-Civil War period is crucial. Then, "Louisiana's business elite had two concerns regarding the labor force: Who would maintain the levees on whose safety the commercial port depended? And who would perform the agricultural labor on the sugar and cotton plantations?" Although "state agents" tried to recruit agricultural labor from abroad, "In the end, whites continued to rely on subordinated black sharecroppers and casual laborers. Lynching and intimidation, plus the lack of a free market for mobile wage labor, effectively confined black laborers to agricultural occupations in the deep South from emancipation through the beginning of the twentieth century."[24] In New Orleans, as well as throughout the Mississippi Delta, the plantation system, "with roots in the seventeenth century," maintained its control over land, financing, and water, while "the new African American communities [remained] trapped inside the boundaries of the plantation complex."[25]

Whereas the black population of the city was only 9 percent when the United States purchased the Louisiana territory from the French, by the twentieth century it had become a "biracial city," which had changed its residential pattern from "mixed neighborhoods" to a radically segregated pattern, created partially during the Jim Crow era and consummated during the New Deal period in which "housing developments" led to "legally enforced segregation," while white flight to "suburbs" accelerated both residential and educational segregation.[26] Moreover, the New Deal was a bad deal for African-American agricultural workers; "it strengthened both traditional incentives and traditional institutions [creating] a positive incentive to Southern planters to demote their workers to the status of casual labor employed only seasonally."[27] Not surprisingly, when Katrina hit, the hollowing out of the African-American labor force produced a statistic of 24.5 percent of the city's residents living below the poverty line (in contrast with a percentage of 13.3 for the country as a whole).[28] And crucially for the effect of the surge on the African Americans in the city, "Low income black neighborhoods in low-lying areas suffered a disproportionate share of the floodwater, while wealthier, whiter neighborhoods on higher land stayed dry."[29]

However, those generalizations, which preoccupied sociological investigations[30] – enumerating impoverished African Americans, wealthier whites, and the locations of the greatest devastation – merely provide abstract data rather than specific experiences. The latter are registered in the faces that are intermittently in focus in Lee's documentary. As Deleuze and Guattari suggest, "The face is a veritable megaphone"[31]; along with the words of the persons who experienced Hurricane Katrina and its aftermath, it conveys the micropolitics of the Katrina event, which Spike Lee's *Levees* provides. Whereas:

> the macropolitics of race in America's twentieth century ... is articulated primarily in policy histories [in which] African Americans have been incorporated in a "story of legal and moral ascent" and in "simplistic accounts of moral progress" ... the micropolitics of race is articulated through practices with which African Americans have sought to manage their day-to-day life worlds in the face of structures and policies of intolerance, exclusion and violence, in "struggles against racial hierarchy."[32]

And the blues aesthetic that permeates Lee's documentary (referred to as a "blues documentary" by one critic)[33] articulates that micropolitics. Although a blues aesthetic is resident in artistic texts that are often associated with mere entertainment, blues genres (as I noted in chapter 1) are understood by many African-American assemblages as "insurrectionary social text[s] [which have the effect of] unsettling a repressive social order."[34]

The blues-inflected documentary film genre that Lee utilized effectively extended Katrina's temporality because of the way film and video constitute "ideal means" to encompass past, present and future "to anticipate historical moments, to suggest interrelationships between the present and the past, and to construct analogies between present and past [and when] critically questioned and framed, recent events are often more immediate and significant than [when they were experienced] as current affairs and live broadcast."[35] To appreciate the political force of Lee's *Levees* we have to see it as an encounter between "documentary time"[36] (an event time that the documentary frames) and historical time, which looks toward an uncertain future. In Lee's film, "the constructed temporality of camera movement, editing, and sound meets with that of the filmed gestures and events, which in turn are marked by the historical moment of their representation."[37]

However, that meeting and marking, which are features of documentaries in general, fail to register a crucial dimension of the experiences of the Katrina event for both the city's residents and the viewers of the documentary. The film's temporal rhythms, conveyed by close-ups of faces and the words of a wide variety of victims who appear, disappear and reappear on screen (punctuated by shots of the devastation of neighborhoods, all surrounded by the varying moods evoked by Terence Blanchard's musical soundtrack) create the film's affective resonances. That assemblage of sound and image constitutes the temporality of the film's form. Its tempo and rhythm deliver the film's affect while it delivers the Lee–Blanchard political version of the Katrina event. As a result, an understanding of how the documentary works requires attention to the interrelationship between the rhythms of Lee's cinematic montage and the rhythms of Blanchard's musical soundtrack.

As is well known, musical genres have often been the vehicles for the articulation of the history of the African-American experience in the United States, and no composition has been as historically comprehensive as Duke Ellington's *Black, Brown and Beige* (introduced in chapter 1), "the story of his people," as Ellington put it. The composition provides "a long historical trajectory of African American musical idioms, while interconnecting the history of the American black experience with the history of their music."[38] To situate the musical contribution to the temporal structure of Lee's documentary, it's instructive to review the temporal structure of Duke Ellington's musical history of the African-American experience and contrast it with Blanchard's musical soundtrack.

The narrative background of Ellington's *Black, Brown and Beige* composition is supplied by his poem in which his character Boola's personal story is interwoven with history as he moves through it. The musical narrative accompanying Boola is linear, beginning with the *Black* section in which Boola begins in Africa, suffers through the Middle Passage and ends up in America where, after taking up Christianity, he approaches a church to which he is irresistibly drawn, represented in a musical composition, "Come Sunday." That piece, which draws from the genre of the spiritual, contains hints of the African-American blues tradition: "short, lyrical statements by solo trombone and trumpet introduce the 'song'" whose structure is a "typical blues style...'flatted fifths.'" The musical at this point resonates with the emotional timbres of an assemblage of African Americans who are kept outside the church, while they support the spirituality in progress inside: "the music holds still, catching its breath [as] 'the blacks outside grunt/subdued approval.'"[39]

When the composition shifts to the *Brown* section,

the rhythms and tonalities of the spiritual follows its historical and musical migration to the blues [as it] features the traditional twelve-bar blues structure...and by the time the narrative moves to *Beige*...the narrative moves from a "weary blues" mood to a hopeful one that is reflected in the intellectual contributions of the Harlem Renaissance and the patriotic contributions of black America's participation in the war effort.[40]

Ultimately, Ellington's piece merges musical history with the history of the African-American experience. For example, in the *Brown* section, "Ellington turns the focus from Boola to specific figures in black history: Crispus Attucks, Barzillai Lew, the Frontages Legion of Free Haitians, Frederick Douglass, Harriet Tubman," and more.[41]

In contrast with Ellington's inter-articulation of musical and black history, which moves in a more or less linear narrative as it treats a historical trajectory of the black experience, the Lee–Blanchard documentary of the Katrina event moves back and forth in both musical and black history as it frames Katrina in the context of the political economy of the black experience in New Orleans. The two dimensions resonate well together, for throughout the documentary there is a homology between the rhythms of the musical soundtrack and the rhythm of Lee's editing. (As Ernest Callenbach puts it, "The rhythm of the music and the rhythm of the cutting concur."[42]) For example, in an interview, Blanchard refers to the silences engendered in the aftermath of the storm, so that all that is heard is the wind. To achieve that effect, his soundtrack reproduces a high-pitched jazz that howls like the wind. Ultimately, Blanchard's musical enactment of the documentary's subtitle is a crucial aspect of how his documentary thinks. His "tragic symphony" (as one commentary puts it) is the musical realization of a requiem mass, which traditionally is a mass for the dead. However, Blanchard's "requiem" is inflected by the history of the African-American soundscape. It is partitioned, chapter by chapter, with different musical prologues from different historical moments. (In the documentary, New Orleans native, the musician Wynton

Marsalis, provides a historical sketch of those moments in a commentary on the musical dimension of New Orleans' life-world.)

Among the soundtrack's musical moments are jazz funerals, which simultaneously celebrate lives and mark deaths. Indeed, much of the imagery in the film is about marking deaths – for example, in several shots of signs on houses that read "dead body inside," and in some of the interviews, which provide testimony about those who did not survive. As Amos Vogel has pointed out, historically the cinematic medium has had a "tendency to avert its eyes before the sight of actual death."[43] Among the reasons for the avoidance is that "of all the transformations of the lived-body in our culture, the event of death seems particularly privileged in its threat to representation."[44] Lee's documentary shows corpses (some recently dead, some in varying states of decay and mummification), as well as signs referring to them. Those moments are interspersed with moments of vibrant (albeit often suffering) life. Lee's editing thus provides a "vigorous contrast between two states of the physical body: the body as lived-body, intentional and animated – and the body as corpse, as flesh unintended, inanimate, static."[45] The showing of the two kinds of bodies is one of the film's dominant temporalities. To put it grammatically, we see bodies who *are* subjects and bodies who *were* subjects, where the latter constitute crucial moments in the visual aspect of Lee's requiem.

At the same time that *Levees* mourns the dead, as it testifies in a chorus of voices of interviewees, who as a whole cut across racial and class lines, it celebrates what New Orleans has been and what of the best of it remains (the overture in chapter 1 provides "lively scenes of the reborn Mardi Gras of 2006"[46]). And while much of Blanchard's soundtrack is elegiac, much of it is joyous – for example the opening of chapter 1 in which we hear Louis Armstrong singing the 1947 song, "Do You Know What it Means to Miss New Orleans?" and the opening and closing chapters in which we hear Fats Domino's "Walking to New Orleans." Along with the temporal shifts, as music from different moments in New Orleans history is summoned, are sections of old film footage. We see early Mardi Gras celebrations in black and white and more recent ones in color.

What ultimately does *Levees* say about New Orleans' future, or its will-have-been? Although aspects of *Levees* offer hints of "individual and collective rebirth,"[47] the warnings to looters, coupled with the violence of vigilantes and the militarization of the police force, which kept many African Americans from fleeing from flooded areas, suggest that the oppressive racial-spatial order of New Orleans retains a disturbing permanence. And as the interviews with residents, many of whom have been relocated to other cities, indicate, the neighborhood culture that had developed from that order, especially that in the Ninth (largely black) Ward, seems unlikely to be restored. Moreover, the coercive way in which families were broken up, as people were dispersed to different cities, harks back (as some interviewees suggest) to the slave period in which plantation owners broke up families, separately selling off husbands, wives, and children. At a minimum, many of the last chapters in *Levees* convey ambivalence. While many are striving to restore New Orleans' musical and carnival culture and other aspects of its traditional lifeworld, many of the bodies that have historically participated in a multitude of New Orleans' cultural practices may never return.

To explore further what New Orleans has been and what the future may hold, I turn to HBO's *Treme*, which in a fictional genre but with a documentary-like aesthetic explores New Orleans past, present, and future in the aftermath of Katrina. Inasmuch as *Treme* is a fictional narrative rather than a documentary, its protagonists are aesthetic rather than ethnographic subjects. Nevertheless, like Lee's ethnographic subjects, writer/director David Simon's characters in *Treme* (many of whom represent actual New Orleans residents) perform both a mapping of the post-Katrina spaces of New Orleans and a mix of temporalities, creating an entanglement between personal biographical time and historical geopolitical time.

Treme

Among the diverse civic spaces within which the meaning of events are negotiated and continually reinterpreted is "the black public sphere," a domain of civic association that is articulated not in the usual white liberal political frame of voting and attendance at (for example, Parent-Teacher Association meetings) but rather in the diverse artistic genres that are very much foregrounded in the HBO series *Treme* and in much of the critical commentary the series has attracted (expanding what I call the *Treme* event).[48] The activities and interpretive dynamics within that sphere, which ponder the aftermath of Katrina, add critical temporal rhythms to the Katrina event, as they summon historical moments and personages that belong to a shadow world behind the world foregrounded in mainstream civic culture. For example, Johari Jabir points to what he sees as a glaring oversight in the Katrina event, the lack of mention of Mahalia Jackson, when "in the first several days following Hurricane Katrina the US media paid tribute to numerous legendary musicians – past and present – who hailed from New Orleans."[49]

In evoking the name of Mahalia Jackson, Jabir provides a Walter Benjamin-like, critical approach to history, a moment of "Messianic time," which has the past shine through at moments in the present. For Jabir, what "flashes up"[50] during the post-Katrina moment is Mahalia Jackson's "Didn't It Rain (1953), which he hears (along with other songs) as "a kind of epistemological 'suite' " which harbors possibilities for assembling a culture of public sharing that challenges the view of America as a totalizing mono culture. Jabir's recollection of the song provides a way to "*learn* some important lessons about race, citizenship, politics, and cultural production."[51] His evocation of

Mahalia Jackson's musical archive sees a "spark of hope" that has smoldered "at the very heart of past events."[52] Jabir goes on to note that "the strong sense of swing throughout [Mahalia's] musical archive" harks back to "a rhythm...held on from slavery." It's a rhythm:

> anchored by a structural organization...[a] sense of time which, when thinking in terms of a performing ensemble, requires a communal instinct and epistemology...that creates the paradox of collective coherence [a paradox because it is]...a reflection on the past and simultaneously a vision of the future; the feeling of being held and being set free in the same moment, so that several things are taking place at the same "time."[53]

Certainly, the *Treme* series, which dwells extensively on the revival and re-inflection of New Orleans' musical traditions, conjures a musical past while envisioning a restored communal future. Although *Treme*'s focus on New Orleans' "unmistakably black and hybrid" cultural practices has drawn criticism for its tendency to "sell the city and its culture" to spur a "tourist economy," it is also seen as contributing to "alternative and emergent possibilities" for the reinvention of the city's cultural life-world.[54] And within *Treme*'s first season, there is a strong critique of the "tourist economy (for example, when the street musician Sonny (Michiel Huisman) mocks tourists from Wisconsin for whom New Orleans music is the iconic "When the Saints Go Marching In"). Ultimately, the "show," as Simon puts it, "is an argument for the city," rather than a focus on "single issues."[55] *Treme*'s first episode is situated three months after Hurricane Katrina. It surveys the devastation of the city while at the same time following the lives of diverse residents as they struggle to come to terms with their losses and manage their presents and futures.

As the episodes and seasons progress, the *Treme* effect is constituted as an encounter between the struggles of its characters to restore or reinvent both their personal and their communal life and the viewers' developing political sense of New Orleans' post-Katrina problems, screened through their own political habitus. It's an encounter of two biographical temporalities. As Simon states:

> A TV show can't hold people and institutions to account like good journalism can. But if I can make you care about a character, I may make you think a little longer about certain dynamics that might cause you to reconsider your own political inertia or your own political myopia. You might be more willing to accept a critique of the prevailing political and social systems.[56]

In attracting the week-to-week allegiance (and, in the best cases, the developing reflectiveness) of its viewers to the series, it is important to note that *Treme* belongs to a television rather than a cinema aesthetic. In the case of a TV series, "the primary object of aesthetic interest...is not the individual piece, but the format."[57] The episodes derive much of their coherence from the formulas that generate them, among which is the continuing participation of the same characters and the progression of their relationships with each other and with the spaces within which they function.[58] And unlike the typical cinematic aesthetic, much of what is offered week-to-week is a background of uneventfulness – the mundane moments of interaction in life-worlds – from which the special events that drive each episode stand out.[59]

Characters (persons situated in different vocational, ethnic, and class positions) and an event (a "second-line" parade) stand out at the beginning of the series, and each provides a different level of temporal depth for the Katrina event. I want therefore to begin my reading of the series with the event, represented as the first second-line parade in post-Katrina New Orleans. We enter the parade from the point of view of two characters, Antoine Batiste (Wendell Pierce) and Davis McClary (Steve Zahn), the former a jazz trombone player who helps to lead the parade and the latter a part-time disk jockey who runs out to join the parade in progress. Their respective locations in a genealogy of musical space (treated below) situate part of the significance of second-line parades, which belong to New Orleans history.

The first post-Katrina second-line parade (so-described by Davis before he runs to join it) articulates well with the death and destruction wrought by Katrina. As Helen Regis remarks, "death haunts the living in New Orleans," a reality that is articulated by the parades which, as she puts it, constitute "a collective space for reflection on the structures that impinge in inner city lives, often shaping the circumstances in which those lives, often too early, come to an end."[60] And, as the parade continually reappears in subsequent *Treme* episodes, the historical depth and multiple dimensions of the "second-line" practice becomes evident. In part through the insertion of older documentary film footage and photographs and in part through conversations about it, the viewers learn to associate that practice with "dance steps," "brass bands," "social clubs," or "social and pleasure clubs," and a dynamic of joining, as watching crowds get swept up in its rhythmic motions, switching from observation to participation.[61]

Inasmuch as the *Treme* series is polydiegetic, its representations of second-line parades belong to one among many of its narratives. In addition to the continuing presence of New Orleans' pluralistic musical cultures throughout the episodes are other narratives, locating characters in fraught familial, social, and erotic relationships, bringing them into encounters that reveal legal worlds, the policing culture, and reactions to official policy at local and federal levels. And all of those relationships transpire in the face of enormous barriers to the city's attempt to restore civic and social life, especially the instability of the population, as many have left and those who have returned cannot reestablish their former life circumstances. Here, heeding the fact that *Treme* is in many ways a "listening text," my emphasis is on the narrative that foregrounds musical culture.[62]

To situate conceptually *Treme*'s musical narrative I summon and treat critically two treatments of music, the philosopher Edmund Husserl's analysis of the temporal structure of a melody in his *Phenomenology of Internal Time Consciousness* and the French cultural minister Jacques Attali's historical genealogy of musical space. Husserl's analysis is restricted to the phenomenology of individual consciousness. He develops two aspects of that phenomenology, "retention," which is a phenomenological expansion of the present, a "longitudinal temporality that extends the 'point-like' instant of the now, and 'protention,' which extends the melody into an anticipation of its future occurrences."[63] For Husserl, music ("melody" in his terms) is an exemplary temporal phenomenon. Even when the sound "dies away," the music is still sensed though "not actually present." It has evoked a "retentional" consciousness that "can remind [the listener] of a past sound."[64]

It is clear, in part through the conversations among the series characters, that the musical narrative in *Treme* is evocative of a past for *Treme*'s characters. And it is also clear that their listening is done in anticipation of a future for the New Orleans soundscape. However, that past has a longitude well beyond the "just past" and the immediate future that shape Husserl's analysis. And, crucially, a model of immanence, which presumes an abstract listener (an individual phenomenological subject) whose presence to music is purely mental, cannot capture the temporal implications of *Treme*'s musical narrative. For the diverse characters in *Treme*, the music they hear evokes different pasts and different anticipations of a future musical culture for New Orleans. Moreover, as the scenes in second-line marches, in clubs, and in the street suggest, the "listeners" are not passive modes of pure consciousness; they are mobilized bodies. They dance and gesture to the resonances of the music and to the movements of those around them. In addition, the venues of the sounds are crucial to how pasts and potential futures are evoked.

As a result, to appreciate *Treme*'s musical narrative, we have to heed the different venues in which the music is heard and responded to, and we have to locate those spaces in a historical trajectory of musical space, noting the differing allegiances of the various characters to alternative musical pasts, alternative hoped-for futures, and their connections with the alternative musical spaces. For that kind of appreciation, a turn to Attali's genealogy of musical space is instructive. For Attali, the temporality of music is a function of technologies of reproduction rather than simply the listening of the phenomenological subject. Because of its repeatability, enabled by recording technology, music, he asserts, is capable of resisting "the ravages of time."[65] And inasmuch as people can buy more recordings than they can listen to at once, repeatable music can "stockpile time."[66]

Attali situates the historically changing temporality of music in a narrative of musical space that precedes as well as incorporates its contemporary repeatability. The story begins with festivals and carnivals, staged by nomadic musicians who perform in the street, a musical space given over to ritual and sacrificial functions that involve participatory crowds. Those functions of music were largely displaced when "the concert hall performance replaced the popular festival [creating]...a gulf between the musicians and audience."[67] And, subsequently, as Attali's narrative continues, the development of recording technologies and the emergence of radio render the walls of the concert hall no longer able to contain musical space. Temporally, the possibilities for repetition that recording technologies lend to music produce "a fundamental change in the relation of man to history because it makes the stockpiling of time possible"[68]; and, spatially, musical discourse becomes "nonlocalizable."[69]

However, Attali recognizes (as Fernand Braudel pointed out before him) that history is "conjunctural."[70] Earlier forms of exchange persist along with newer ones. Articulating that view with musical history, Attali writes, "Music, like cartography, records the simultaneity of conflicting orders."[71] Doubtless, the musical cultures of New Orleans provide an exemplary case of that simultaneity. *Treme*'s first season introduces musician/protagonists who represent different moments in the historical spatio-temporality that Attali maps, and those differences provide a persistent theme in subsequent seasons.

As I suggested in my treatment of the Lee–Blanchard documentary of the Katrina event, *Levee*, New Orleans' musical history is located "in the context of the political economy of the black experience in New Orleans." In moving to a consideration of the musical narrative in *Treme*, I want to complicate that political economy by noting its fraught relationships with geographies and biographies (and thus with what I want to call moral economy). Conflicts over musical styles in the *Treme* series – beginning in season one – are effectively located within the moral economy–political economy divide. Music is arguably *Treme*'s main character. As it is articulated though diverse protagonists, the most temporally significant narrative thread within which it is thematized involves the relationship between Albert "Big Chief" Lambreaux (Clarke Peters) and his son Delmond (Rob Brown), where Albert positions himself as the guardian of the moral economy of New Orleans music and Delmond is associated with modern, commercially oriented jazz. For Albert, the percussive, Indian version of jazz is a cultural treasure with ontological depth and a ritual function (primarily to be performed in the street during Mardi Gras by elaborately costumed "Indians"), while Delmond, at least at the outset of the series, is a performer (trumpeter) of a commoditized modern jazz in concert venues (Lincoln Hall in New York primarily). Generational time is thus articulated with historical time. Albert seeks to preserve a cultural past, while his son is associated with a commercial present.

The moral-versus-political economy divide that the father–son conflict exemplifies needs conceptual specification. As I have put it elsewhere, " 'Moral economy' is an inter-discursive field in which cultural imperatives and ongoing negotiations shape what is regarded as acceptable versus unacceptable forms of exchange and what kinds of persons are eligible as licit traders and/or consumers."[72] The *political* economy, insofar as it is institutionalized within society, is the authoritative, officially sanctioned field of exchangeable things. As the boundary between the two economies is destabilized at various historical moments, cultural authorities weigh in diverse media. One such historical moment is illustrated by Joyce Appleby, who points to the period in the seventeenth century when sustained economic development in England created a challenge to the old "moral economy" of "production and sustenance." "[T]he daily round of tasks sustained by a divine rationale" was being displaced by a newly emerging subject – an "individual" – who "had become subsumed in a depersonalized aggregation."[73] As the prior "moral universe" became destabilized, cultural authorities (primarily clergy) began pamphleting both in favor and against the depersonalized system of exchange (for example, one who insisted that "the freedom to set prices was a petty, pretentious assertion, incompatible with the laws of man and God"[74]).

As *Treme*'s seasons progressed, the division between Albert Lambreaux and his son Delmond attenuated. Initially, in his role as a cultural icon involved in a "counter-drive" to the commoditization of music, Albert resists performing in a musical style that renders the music as an exchangeable good (as Igor Kopytoff puts it, culture is a "counterdrive" that inhibits the "potential onrush of commoditization"[75]), and his preferred venue of performance is the street, the space of festival and ritual that preceded music's migration into the confined spaces (clubs and concert halls) of musical commoditization where, as Attali points out, the ritual aspect of music had largely disappeared (although New Orleans' funerals, second lines and Mardi Gras parades defy that narrative).[76] However, as the *Treme* seasons progress, Albert begins to lose his contempt for Delmond's musical vocation and the spatial practices within which it flourishes. At the same time, Delmond develops a passion for New Orleans' musical heritage and begins working on a temporally hybrid music that incorporates his father's traditional/ethnic, percussive musical rhythms within aspects of modern jazz to preserve the embodied resonances of the former and emphasize the swing, dance-provoking aspects of the latter. By the time *Treme*'s last season is underway (before Albert dies of cancer), Albert agrees to perform in non-street venues with Delmond's ensemble.

Kopytoff suggests that, "In every society there are things that are publicly precluded from being commoditized."[77] However, as *Treme* makes evident, New Orleans' ethnoscape complicates the concept of the public. *Treme* dramatizes New Orleans' plurality of publics. Albert's "public" is a marginalized counter-public that resists the musical commoditization that is welcomed by others. As Delmond migrates back into his father's counter-public, the musical collaboration between father and son draws him physically back to New Orleans as well, while at the same time summoning Albert into a musical modernity that honors the past, produces a different present, and strives to summon New Orleans jazz into a future that brings disparate publics together.

Conclusion: Katrina's Will-Have-Been

Spike Lee's *Levees* and David Simon's *Treme* testify to what much of the mediascape treated all too briefly and sketchily. They reveal that among the major effects of the Katrina event was the death, dislocation, trauma, and precariousness visited on black lives. Clyde Woods captures that aspect of the event succinctly: "The disaster surrounding Hurricane Katrina revealed the impaired contemporary social vision of every segment of society. Despite mountains of communication and surveillance devices

America was still shocked by the revelation of impoverish-ment, racism, brutality, corruption, and official neglect in a place it thought it knew intimately."[78]

Woods's use of the past tense for America's shock raises some pressing questions, which reference the endurance of the Katrina event. Does that shock continue to be regis-tered with "America's" mediascape and is it still present in the affective temporalities (the ongoing effects of trauma, dislocation, and suffering)? With respect to the first ques-tion, Katrina can be construed as a media subject under the rubric "black lives matter." The racism, brutality and official neglect to which Woods refers in his reflections on the Katrina event are once again foregrounded in popular media in response to the shooting of unarmed African Americans by police officers in Ferguson, Missouri, Madison, Wisconsin, Charleston, South Carolina, and Bal-timore, Maryland (and the strangulation of an African American by a police officer in Staten Island, New York), especially after grand juries failed to indict the officers involved in the Ferguson and Staten Island cases. Signifi-cantly, one internet outlet reported that the protesters of the shooting of the unarmed teenager, Michael Brown, in Ferguson referred to the event as "Obama's Katrina." ("This is Obama's Katrina, and he ain't doing s**t!" – an answer to the question about Katrina's continuing affective resonances.[79]) Consolidating the four episodes of police violence against African Americans (the list grows as I write), the media's frequent referencing of Katrina effectively renders Katrina as what Karl Mannheim famously called a "paradigmatic experience," the kind of experience that continues to serve as a "measuring rod for human conduct."[80]

In terms of the temporality that the recent Katrina refer-ences evoke, Walter Benjamin provides us with a model (described in chapter 1). Displacing the linear narrative of history (the continuum from past to present) with episodes of shock, he refers to moments when the past, which "carries a temporal index...flashes up at a moment of danger."[81] In terms of the ethico-political questions that the evocation of Katrina raise, Judith Butler provides us with insights that also challenge a linear reading of the event's violence. She puts into question how we define an injurable or precarious life, how as a result we grieve for some rather than others, and how our perceptions are, ultimately, unknowing (predicated on norms that tend to be accepted unreflectively). As she puts it, "The epistemological capacity to apprehend a life is partially dependent on that life being produced by norms that qualify it as a life, or, indeed, as part of life."[82] Moreover, "apprehension" is not mere perception for Butler: "The precarity of life imposes an obligation on us."[83] Heeding Butler's couplet, apprehension, and obligation, I return to David Simon's remark on the temporal structure of a television series and its potential for creating consciousness about the political inertia of prevailing institutions and policy. He suggests that once a life's complicated habitus is apprehended, the obligation to regard it sympathetically can follow. Perhaps Spike Lee's *Levees* and David Simon's *Treme*, both of which allow viewers to live virtually (for extended periods) with the precarity of particular black protagonists who have endured the Katrina event, militate in favor of the recognition of the "ethical weight" of black lives.

Lee and Simon are professional documentarians. While doubtless their work has had a revelatory impact on what many Americans perceive about the country's racial divide, much of what is now becoming apparent about the precariousness of black lives is made evident through the intrusion of the "citizen documentary."[84] While it was photography, in the hands of a professional journalist/ writer, Jacob Riis, which made the tenement life of poor Americans available to a mass audience by documenting the squalid living conditions in New York City slums in the 1880s.[85] it is the handheld video recorder and/ or smartphone-recording application that captures the ways that "law enforcement" personnel disproportionately harass, oppress, and murder black citizens.

In a sense, the photographs in Riis's exposure of tenement life contained their own futurity because, as an enactment of Riis's belief that images "would have the power to expose the tenement-house problem in a way that his textual reporting could not do alone,"[86] his photographic event helped to inaugurate a new use of photographic technology, a utilization of its ability to shock sensibilities by its stark exposure of harsh living conditions. His photographs were thus "metapictures,"[87] images that encourage the development of a new genre in visual culture. The development of video technology is also an important event; it supplies a similar technology-temporality story. Once the video recorder migrated from the private to the public sphere, its application changed from its facilitation of family viewing to the exposure of public events, and, as Rune Saugmann Andersen points out, its potential for investigative journalism and public policy was spurred by two notable events of video capture: "the Zapruder video, showing the assassination of US President Kennedy [and]...the LAPD beating of Rodney King." "It became clear," he adds, "that the video could not only document what was already deemed to become an event of international significance but also transform events from local to international."[88] Thus, like Riis's photographs of New York slums, the Zapruder and Rodney King videos contained their own futurity.

That futurity, realized of late in the video capture of police killings of unarmed African Americans, is part of our present. As has become evident, the video images documenting the suffering of the black victims of Hurricane Katrina and of the slow federal response to their plight turned what was a remote event for most Americans into a racial sublime (in Immanuel Kant's sense, an episode of enormous magnitude that challenges understandings of the relationship between subjectivity and the world of experience).[89] What was witnessed was what *Newsweek* magazine termed "the other America," an unprecedented visibility in which black victims "commanded the center

stage of national attention [a moment of]...critical attention [that] marks both a rupturing of America's racial
discourse and the deleterious effects of the nation's pre-
Katrina racial order,"[90] which (as Walter Benjamin would
put it) "flashes up at a moment of danger."

Similarly, the democratization of video capacity (most
pervasively in smartphone applications) is radially extending the impact of that racial sublime. As the freelance
documentation of the widespread abuse of black citizens
by law enforcement personnel proceeds, the magnitude of
the precariousness of the lives of African Americans
becomes a daunting challenge to the national imagination.
As moments in Ferguson, Baltimore, Charleston, Staten
Island, Arlington (and other cities) shift from a local to a
national imaginary, it becomes evident in a way not previously appreciated by white America that (as Michael Eric
Dyson puts it) "the lived experience of race feels like terror
for black folk."[91] The concept of the sublime helps me to
shape chapters 4 and 5, which focus among other things
on the sweatshop and weapons sublimes respectively.

4
Keeping Time: The Rhythms of Work and the Arts of Resistance

Introduction: The Dance and Critical Thinking

In his first lecture on "Reason and Existenz," Karl Jaspers credits Kierkegaard's and Nietzsche's questioning of the way the concept of reason had been rendered in the history of philosophy and offers this understatement: "Their thinking created a new atmosphere."[1] I want to note that the atmosphere persists and to enjoin a trope that they both employed: the dance. As Jaspers puts it, "In the last decade of his life Nietzsche, in ever changing forms, used the dance as a metaphor for his thought, where it is original," and he quotes Kierkegaard's remark: "I have trained myself to be able to dance in the service of thought."[2] Jaspers appropriates the Nietzschean and Kierkegaardian insights in order to re-inflect philosophical discourse. He suggests that the idea of the dance helped philosophy to exit from self-enclosed models of reason and rationality.

Heeding that insight, my intellectual practice has been to regard Nietzsche's and Kierkegaard's interventions as an inspiration not only for critical philosophical practice but also for exiting from legitimating discourses of political conciliation, those discourses that occult the fault lines in the body politic. For example, in a reading of Cormac McCarthy's novel *Blood Meridian*, I refer to the importance for the history of philosophy of Nietzsche's gloss (in *The Birth of Tragedy*) on the self as an inter-animation of the Apollonian and Dionysian energies, the former being detached and form-giving and the latter being both creative and destructive. In Nietzsche's view, such productive tension was lost when philosophy was re-inflected by Plato's Socrates, whose mission was to suppress the tension in order to make existence appear rationally intelligible and thereby self-justifying. The new post-Socratic "mood" (as Jaspers would have it) creates a thinking space to question older models of reason, all of which privilege particular forms of institutionalized authority rather than yielding an unimpeachable universality of thought. Samuel Beckett understood that well. He too questions self-enclosed models of reason, using his aesthetic subject, Belacqua (a character borrowed from Dante), in a story in the collection *More Pricks than Kicks*. At one point, Belacqua, involved in a seduction, had "No sooner...opened his project than she applied for his reasons." The text goes on:

> forewarned by the study he has made of his catspaw mind, he was able to pelt her there and then with the best diligent enquiry could provide: Greek and Roman reasons, Sturm and Drang reasons, reasons metaphysical, aesthetic, erotic and chemical, Empedocles of Agrigentum and John of the Cross reasons, in short all but the true reasons, which did not exist, at least not for purposes of conversation.[3]

To return to the dance: in my reading of Cormac McCarthy's novel, I suggest that the dance is a trope with which one can displace authoritative and imposed choreographies (the entrenched *reasons* of self-displacing corporeal hegemonies) with self-actualizing movement. Specifically, in my reading of *Blood Meridian*, I emphasize the dance trope to think through the sharp contrast between the filmmaker John Ford's and Cormac McCarthy's perspectives on the political evolution of the American West. I argue that in Ford's film *My Darling Clementine* (1946), a dance scene has more significance than the famous gunfight at the O.K. Corral. Toward the end of the film narrative, there is a celebration of the building of a church. In the scene, it is only partly built; it has wooden beams and an open framework with a wooden platform as its base. Onto that platform step the two key characters, Wyatt Earp and his intended, Clementine, to begin a dance whose significance is underscored by a musical soundtrack that conveys the promise of a happy conjugal/familial future. The effect of the scene – as is the case in so many of Ford's familial bonding scenes – is to moralize a West that is being incorporated into the Euro-American ethnogenesis (the whitening of the American continent) to positively sanction the Euro-American expansion rather than, for example, pondering the costs (paid by indigenous nations) of the violence associated with that expansion (as he does in his *Cheyenne Autumn* in 1964).[4]

In sharp contrast is Cormac McCarthy's novel, which also enlists the trope of the dance but with a very different valence from Ford's. His character, Judge Holden (a huge, violent, and very cerebral man), is figured as a dancer when at one point, as the Glanton gang (a group of marauders who kill and pillage, collecting Indian and Mexican scalps to sell to local mayors on both sides of the US–Mexican border) is seated around a fire, one character, the "ex-priest," says, "God, the man is a dancer."[5] Just as Nietzsche, in many places, affirms the value of the dance – e.g., "I would believe only in a god who could dance"[6] – the judge himself valorizes the dance: "What man would not be a dancer if he could, said the judge. It's a great thing, the dance."[7] Subsequently, in a soliloquy, the judge has more to say about the dance as he ponders the rationale for the orchestration of events:

> This is an orchestration for an event. The participants will be apprised of their roles at the proper time...As the dance

is the thing with which we are concerned and contains complete within itself its own arrangement and history and finale there is no necessity that the dancers contain these things within themselves as well. In any event the history of all is not the history of each nor indeed the sum of those histories.[8]

The point of this passage – as Nietzsche would have appreciated – is that subjectivity is epiphenomenal to creative action. To invent a preexisting subject is to moralize by inventing and privileging a subject behind the action. However distasteful the judge's violent actions may be – he is an imperturbable murderer (reminiscent of Albert Camus' Caligula, who remarks that what he admires most about himself is his imperturbability) – his point articulates with McCarthy's: there is no privileged historical agency. The landscape has witnessed violent encounters, driven by enmities. It contains numerous unrecorded histories and it privileges none. Contrary to Ford's embrace of legitimating legends, McCarthy offers "reality." In place of fraudulent destinies, he offers the contingencies of encounter. In place of moralizing what has already been institutionalized, his novel invites ethical reflection. Jaspers' Nietzsche- and Kierkegaard-inspired (and McCarthy's Nietzsche-inspired) privileging of "the dance" drives much of the thinking in this chapter, which (among other things) sorts critical, self-actualizing movement from non-critical, imposed choreographies.

Choreographies

It can take an awkward moment for us to realize that some of our movements and gestures are choreographed. This one took place in the fall of 1966, during my first semester as an assistant professor of political science at the University of Hawai'i. It was habitual for me and two of my colleagues (I'll give them fitting pseudonyms: "Stan Laurel") and "Oliver Hardy") to head to the student cafeteria for mid-morning coffee. Typically, as we reached our office building on the return trip and were about to mount the stairs to our second-floor offices, "Stan" and I would sashay leftward to let "Oliver," a very large man whose weight roughly equaled the sum of mine and Stan's, to turn rightward to use the first-floor men's room (doubtless because his bladder was under more pressure than ours). One day, Oliver didn't have to go, and as Stan and I made our usual leftward move, he went straight ahead and knocked us both down.

My anecdote references a piece of choreography that was part of an unsponsored routine of everyday life. However, much of the movement of bodies everywhere is choreographed by aspects of power, authority and control – forms of coordination and mastery for which both Michel Foucault and Henri Lefebvre summoned the concept of dressage. Foucault attributes the inauguration of dressage to "the classical age," which:

> discovered the body as object and target of power. It is easy enough to find signs of the attention then paid to the body – to the body that is manipulated, shaped, trained, which obeys, responds, becomes skillful and increases its forces...which was constituted by a whole set of regulations and by empirical and calculated methods relating to the army, the school and the hospital, for controlling or correcting the operations of the body.[9]

And Lefebvre saw it as a pervasive aspect of modernity, a system through which humans "break themselves in like animals...one breaks-in another living human by making them repeat a certain act." Like Foucault, he saw it as a legacy of "the military model," which got extended as a "rhythm through all phases of our temporality."[10]

Certainly, the contemporary choreography of the body is responsive to a significant historical change, which Paul Virilio has pointed out. He suggests that the French

Revolution did not end subjection in general. What was a
revolution against the "*constraint to immobility*" [11] of the
monarchical-sponsored aristocratic society shifted its modality. With the birth of the modern state, the "*freedom of
movement*,"[12] of the early days of the revolution was converted through the force of state power to an "*obligation
to mobility*."[13] Subsequently (as I have noted elsewhere),
"commercial forces have been at least as involved in the
mobilization of bodies [and their choreographed gestures]
as the state."[14] Accordingly as E. P. Thompson points out,
"already in 1700, the familiar landscape of disciplined
industrial capitalism, with the time-sheet, the time-keeper,
the informers and fines" had emerged.[15] And as various
industries developed, especially "the textile mills and the
engineering workshops where the new time discipline was
most rigorously imposed...the contest over time became
most intense."[16] By the "third generation," workers became
less quiescent. Rather than blindly following the imposed
order of time-discipline, they made demands for "overtime
and time-and-a-half. They had accepted the categories of
their employers and learned to fight back within them. They
had learned their lesson that time is money, only too well."[17]

Nevertheless, in part because industries have become
highly mobile, able to flee from places where they encounter worker resistance and recruit a more docile labor force
elsewhere, coercive forces (now globally dispersed) remain
dominant. Here, inspired especially by some observations
by Frantz Fanon, my focus is mainly on the way postcolonial global capital mobilizes captured bodies in enterprises
in what was formerly called the "underdeveloped" Third
World (in effect, a re-colonization). Turning in the conclusion of his classic, *The Wretched of the Earth*, to a call to
resist a re-subjugation of the newly liberated postcolonial
peoples, Fanon insists that "we" must "stop talking about
output, and intensification, and the rhythm of work" and
must look elsewhere than to Europe in order to "work out
new concepts and try to set afoot a new man."[18]

In reaction to the discourse of economic development
that government functionaries and academics elaborated

in support of "First World"-dominated global capitalism in the mid-twentieth century, Fanon urges the peoples of the Third World to exit from the "caravan" and reject the concept of catching up, a process "dragging men towards mutilation...imposing upon the brain rhythms which very quickly obliterate and wreck it [a process]...used to push man around, to tear him away from himself or from his privacy, to break and kill him."[19]

Among the conditions of possibility for Fanon's polemic on behalf of the suborned, rhythm-induced victims of a predatory global capitalism is the discourse of nineteenth-century political economy, within which the working body is introduced into the problem of value. Foucault identifies the relevant perpetrators, giving David Ricardo's analysis "decisive importance" for "singl[ing] out in a radical fashion, for the first time, the worker's energy, toil, and time that are bought and sold, and the activity that is at the origin of the value of things."[20] Moreover, with Ricardo, the problem of value is lent a significant long-term temporality; his thinking "made possible the articulation of economics on history."[21] As applied to the working body, it fell to Ricardo's contemporary, Thomas Malthus, to provide an anthropology of that temporality/history. Addressing the "biological properties of a human species," Malthus implicates the hardships of labor. For Malthus, "The positivity of economics is situated in an anthropological hollow. *Homo oeconomicus* is not the human being who represents his own needs to himself, and the objects capable of satisfying them; he is the human being who spends, wears out, and wastes his life in evading the imminence of death."[22]

Taking off from Fanon's observations, which move the story of the oppressed working body from a Euro-centered problem of political economy to a global, colonial problematic, Stefano Harney moves forward in history to note:

> an important difference between the rhythm of work Fanon is describing and the historical institution of Fordist and Taylorist rhythms of the assembly line. The Fordist and Taylorist factory had an outside, however unstable and

unjust. Control of cooperation at work was given up, but
was supposed to return individually, at least for white men
and settlers, in politics, in rights, and votes. In the European model imposed on the colonies, there was no return.
The rhythm was all in factory, field, and mine, on the ship,
the road, and the rail, in the shop and the house. Or at
least, this was the system's intent. In this sense the colony
was the first social factory.[23]

A Post-Fordist, Fordist-Looking Future: Alex Rivera's *Sleep Dealer*

In his film *Sleep Dealer* (2008), Alex Rivera moves the
story of the imposed work rhythms of the "social factory"
into a future, which is (in his words) "a future that really
could be five minutes from now."[24] The setting of the film
is a militarized and exploitive boundary control over water
access within Mexico and a totally closed border between
the United States and Mexico. Two protagonists with different temporal imaginaries are featured at the outset of
the film, which opens in the small village of Santa Ana in
rural Mexico where the Cruz family – except for one son,
Memo (Luis Fernando Peña), who is busy hacking into the
world's communication network – is at dinner. After
Memo is summoned to the table, his mother tells him and
his father, Miguel (José Concepción Macías), that they
need more water. The two trek to a nearby fenced and
heavily guarded reservoir, where under the sights of a
machine gun, they have to feed money into a machine to
gain access to the water.

On the return trip to Casa Cruz, they have a telling
conversation. Frustrated with the oppressive situation in
which the Del Rio Corporation in San Diego owns the
water and keeps raising the fee for access to the reservoir,
Memo asks, "Why are we here?" to which his father
replies – in a grammar that locates the future in the past
– "Because here we had a future." I have addressed such

seemingly paradoxical grammatical constructions elsewhere, observing that the problem of being present to both
the past and the future is managed by subjects through
"grammatical proprieties."[25] Accordingly, to make sense
of Miguel's grammatical construction about a past future,
we can turn to analyses that treat the relationship between
grammar and temporality – for example, Reinhart Koselleck's, who in his *Futures Past* points out that it is precisely
"linguistic activity" through which "historical events,"
which bear on subjects' presence to their historical experiences, can be rendered intelligible (in this case, the events
through which a territory that was once locally controlled
became absorbed into a network of a coercively enforced
global capitalism).[26]

Addressing the relationship between such "linguistic
activities" and global capitalism, Franco Berardi, focusing
on the role of financialization, points to the "the rhythmic
disturbance provoked by semio-capital"[27] (i.e., the discursive legitimations accompanying global capitalism), which
impose a "digital rhythm into the social body."[28] Putting
it hyperbolically, he writes, "Financial parthenogenesis
sucks down and dries up every social and linguistic potency,
dissolving the products of human activity especially of
collective semiotic activity."[29] For Berardi, the antidote is
a turn to the arts, specifically poetry, in order to "play a
new game: the game of reactivating the social body" – to
create a space to "tune into a shared vibration."[30] Heeding
Berardi's conceptual gesture but emphasizing the embodied aspect of such attunement, my emphasis in what
follows is on music, dance, and cinema rather than poetry.
My investigation pursues examples of the challenges that
bodily counter-rhythms create for those imposed in the
global factory.

Turning back to the venue of Rivera's film, at the level
of macropolitics the effects of global capitalism on the
locales throughout Latin America are well known. For
example, since the early 2000s, "Every single day tens of
thousands of people pour into clothing factories all over

Central America . These workers – teenagers, sisters, broth-
ers, mothers, fathers, grandparents, students, musicians,
artists, and activists – often live in cramped, makeshift
homes, with corrugated roofs, dirt floors, and little running
water or electricity."[31] Large retail enterprises, the largest
being Walmart, are at the top of a power pyramid, deter-
mining through a process of pitting "vendor against vendor,
country against country, whether the work provided in one
sector will be sustained in the long term."[32] To put the
issue in macropolitical terms, as one investigation into
global "supply chains" expresses it, "a huge differential in
sheer scale and buying power... exists between large retailers in the US and manufacturers and suppliers [across
borders] lower down the supply chain [thus]... Walmart
can say, 'This is our margin, this is what we're going to
make. Who's going to service us?' "[33]

At the micropolitical level are the individual workers
who must struggle to cope with working conditions and
job security, both of which depend on the extent to which
forms of cross-border solidarity can be effected (for
example, through anti-sweatshop campaigns[34]) in the face
of the control over global markets and thus the spaces and
nature of work. That level of experience and political
struggle is documented in investigations that employ ethnographic methods (following for example such workers
as Isabel Reyes, a garment worker in Honduras who "sews
sleeves onto 1,200 shirts every single day," while working
ten-hour days for "$35 a week").[35]

Rivera's film treats a different cross-border problematic
(and ultimately solidarity) in a futuristic rendering of the
age of contemporary global capitalism in which we witness
the situation of a high demand by diverse enterprises (agricultural, industrial, commercial, and household) for inex-
pensive (and often illegal) Mexican labor within the United
States, accompanied by growing political pressure to police
the border to keep the illegal workers out. His film presents
a highly plausible, technologically enabled future in which
Mexican workers can reside in Mexico and work in the

United States without crossing the border. However, in contrast with the sterile and bloodless discourses available in treatises on global political economy, the film treats specific individual human consequences as it mobilizes bodies ("aesthetic subjects"[36]) whose experiences and trajectories of movement map the human consequences of that political economy as it has devolved into a plausible future. After using visuals to contrast the powerful Del Rio Corporation (situated in a tall building in San Diego), which owns the reservoir in Memo's village, with the small single-level home of the Cruz family (in the dry and dusty village of Santa Ana: see Figures 4.1 and 4.2), the film narrative follows two of the key aesthetic subjects, Memo Cruz and Rudy Ramirez (Jacob Vargas). After the surveillance arm of the corporation registers Memo's hacking

Figure 4.1 The Del Rio Corporation

Figure 4.2 Casa Cruz

into its web site, it identifies Memo's home as a center of "aqua terrorism" and sends a weaponized drone, piloted by Rudy Ramirez, to attack the Cruz home.

In addition to controlling workspace, the Del Rio Corporation exercises its hegemony through global media. On a global television channel, it prefaces the drone strike on Casa Cruz with a brief bio of their drone pilot, Ramirez. The video presents his matriculation as a pilot, his military patrimony (as both parents had military careers), and includes an interview with his proud parents to render Ramirez's story as an example of the realization of the "American dream." It then cuts to real-time broadcasting of Ramirez's first mission against the "aqua terrorists." Memo, who is watching television with his brother at his brother's home, sees what is about to happen, a drone strike on Casa Cruz, and runs to warn his family. He is too late. The viewer sees the drone destroy the house and then exterminate a wounded Miguel Cruz, as he crawls from his burning home.

Ironically, the hegemony of the world of global capital has mesmerized Memo as much as it has Rudy. After the destruction of his parents and home, the saddened and chastened Memo heads to Tijuana in search of the version of the "American dream" he has evinced as he monitored the world outside his village. After a misadventure in Tijuana (a mugging in which his money is stolen), "The City of the Future," as it is characterized on a billboard that Memo sees while entering the city on a bus, Memo is fitted with nodes by Luz Martinez (Leonor Varela), a woman he meets on the bus. Luz sells stories on the web and moonlights as a "coyotek," one who implants the nodes on bodies to prepare the labor for a factory that hooks up their workers through their nodes so they can be jacked into a bio-cyberspace to work remotely in the United States – as cab drivers, construction workers, and childcare nannies (indeed almost every occupational category) – while their bodies remain in Tijuana. A voice-over in the high-tech, Fordist-looking factory, where an

Figure 4.3 A futuristic Fordist factory

assembly line of workers are hooked up to their virtual jobs (Figure 4.3), announces, "We give the U.S. what they've always wanted, all the work without the workers." US corporate hegemony has created a virtual Bantustan in Tijuana.

The film has a polydiegetic structure. While one of its narrative threads focuses on Luz's decision to tell Memo's story on her online story blog and on the romance that develops between her and Memo, as his body becomes as attractive to her as his story, another is focused on the way that the factory's work destroys the bodies of the laborers as it follows Memo's increasing exhaustion. Shortly after he has begun working remotely in San Diego, helping to erect the steel scaffolding for a building under construction, Memo's mother, with whom he is in contact on Skype, notices that he doesn't look well and asks him about his diet. Memo's voice-over acknowledges what he won't tell his mother: "How can I tell her the truth? I was just figuring it out for myself. My energy was being drained – sent far away. What happened to the river [dammed up to create the Del Rio Corporation's guarded reservoir] was happening to me." In one scene, what was happening to Memo was consummated in the case of another worker whose immobile body is carried out of the factory after he has collapsed. Memo, who helps transport the man, is told to get right back to work. The coercively imposed, exhaustion-producing work rhythms of the futuristic Fordist factory are then highlighted at a point at which Memo becomes delirious and briefly unhooks himself. An automated voice from the surveillance system tells him that he has been idle for ten seconds and will have his pay adjusted accordingly. It is well known that powerful urban centers (famously figured by Fernand Braudel as whirl-pools) suck products from remote areas. In Rivera's film, the energy of the remote Mexican laborers is being sucked from diverse places within the United States. Memo, rec-ognizing what is happening, decides that his future does not belong in that virtual border-crossing factory.

An Aesthetic Intervention: Storytelling

While the film itself articulates a politics of aesthetics, constituted through the way the relations among its aes-thetic subjects mobilize a critique of the labor inequalities and health afflictions that a policed border between the United States and Mexico creates, the film's other narrative thread, which follows the relationship between Memo and Luz, provides another politics of aesthetics through its focus on storytelling. After Luz posts the story about Memo on the web (which provides a breach of borders that border policing has not inhibited), Rudy Ramirez sees it and realizes he has been used by the Del Rio Corporation to destroy an innocent family. He decides to cross the border in person in search of Memo to try and make amends. Luz's story, which alerts and touches Ramirez, brings him face to face with Memo and ultimately enables a productive cross-border solidarity between them. To compensate for the atrocity of the drone strike on Casa Cruz, Ramirez operates his drone again, this time sending it to blow up the dam in Santa Ana, releasing the water for the free use of Memo's home community.

Although Luz's storytelling (which she markets elec-tronically), like the virtual factory in Tijuana, makes use of the virtual space of the web, it nevertheless contrasts with the connection-engendered atrocities visited on the virtual labor force. Rather than creating the exhausting choreography of the virtual factory, it creates a solidarity-producing resistance to corporate control and the hegemony of capitalism articulated through the captivation effect of the "American dream." As Rivera puts it, "The technologies that in the beginning were forces of alienation become converted into tools that serve the characters in a deep and hopeful way, even if it's just for a few moments." And speaking more generally about the significance of cinema, he says, "Film...informs the way we see the world and therefore the way we imagine politics, the way we debate the future of the world."[37] Inspired by Rivera's insights into the critical interventions of the arts, I turn to an examination of the differential role of cinema and other arts in either supporting or resisting the dressage involved in the imposed rhythms of labor.

Artistic Choreographies: Suborned and Resistant Bodies

Cinema

Who can forget the hilarious scenes in the satirical critique of the technology of efficiency of the Fordist industrial factory in Charlie Chaplin's *Modern Times* (1936)? The film, which begins with an image of a clock, moves to the factory's machine-driven command structure, proceeds to footage of a speeded-up assembly line of frantic workers (with Chaplin as himself at the front of the line), and presents the *reductio ad absurdum* of the coercively imposed rhythms of the Fordist factory. *Modern Times* stands out as a critique of industrial capitalism in an era in which Hollywood (in the first half of the twentieth century) was more prone to producing capitalism-friendly films that celebrated the pursuit of success and upward mobility rather than critiquing inequality and the hardships of labor. Exemplary was King Vidor's *An American Romance*, a celebration of the American dream, whose narrative structure followed an immigrant, Steve Dangos (Brian Donlevy), from his arrival on Ellis Island through his employment, beginning as a miner who graduates to steelworker, through his ascension to foreman, and thence to an automobile entrepreneur who is able to use the knowledge he gained as a steelworker to invent a safe, steel-framed car. In the film, "America" is a land of opportunity, and its mines and factories are spaces of upward mobility, rather than arenas extracting labor while shortening lives through exhaustion and morbidity.

It's instructive to contrast the choreography of the body of King Vidor's Steve Dangos in *An American Romance* with that of Charlie Chaplin in *Modern Times*. Vidor's film belongs to the classic cinema genre in which moving bodies were merely vehicles of the film narrative. As Vincent Amiel puts it, the tendency was "to abandon the body's density for the exclusive profit of its functionality."[38] In contrast, in much of critically oriented cinema, the body is no longer a mere support of the plot. For example, in the case of the films of Buster Keaton, Luc Bresson, and John Cassavetes – the bases for Amiel's analysis (and I would add Charlie Chaplin) – the character's "bursts and rhythms of action escape...the suppositions of a preconceived instrumentalization."[39] The films restore to the body "the complexity of its own determinations."[40] For example, neither Charlie Chaplin in *Modern Times* nor Buster Keaton in *College* (1927) is absorbed into the choreographies of work (in Chaplin's case) nor is the masculine ideal articulated in diverse college sports (in Keaton's).

Watching Chaplin's *Modern Times*, the viewer is doubtless prone to seeing the extraordinarily speeded-up factory work rhythms (which Chaplin subverts with comical moments of inattention and extraneous, time-consuming gestures) as an exaggeration of the time-pressure of the

factory's assembly line. However, life in some contemporary Chinese factories imitates Chaplin's fiction. For
example in the spray-paint division of the Huangwu No.
2 Toy Factory, which supplies Walmart and Dollar General-Toy, the workers' "assigned production goal" for the
more experienced workers requires them to "paint 8,920
small toy pieces a day, or 1,115 per hour...one every 3.23
seconds in order to earn $3.45 for the eight hours," while
a newer worker has a reprieve: "7,200 small pieces in eight
hours, or 900 pieces an hour...one every four seconds.
Workers who fail to reach their goal for the shift will see
their wages drop to...$1.23 to $1.48, and 15 to 18 cents
an hour. The work pace is furious and unimaginably
relentless," and the shifts last much longer than eight
hours – often 15 to 19 hours a day, seven days a week,
repeating the same furious motion 10,000 times a day, "[a]
constant repetition [that] wears off their skin, leaving them
with sore, blistered and bleeding hands and fingers."[41]

While some treatises on global political economy function as apologies for the oppressive conditions in the
Chinese (and other factories) – by focusing for example
on a comparison between the remuneration in sweatshops
and the average remuneration of other forms of labor[42] – a
challenging micropolitical perspective is available not only
in academic monographs but also in documentary films.[43]
Among the most notable documentaries that deal with
China's sweatshops is Lotta Ekelund and Kristina Bjurl-
ing's *Santa's Workshop: Inside China's Slave Labour Toy
Factories* (2004), which employ 90 percent women (many
of whom cannot afford living outside and end up living
"within the confines of the factory walls in virtual prison
cell accommodation or even sleep on the factory floor
itself") because, as the manager puts it, "They're easier to
manage."[44] And among the documentaries that deal with
Tijuana's sweatshops is Vicky Funari and Sergio De La
Torre's *Maquilapolis: City of Factories* (2006), a product
of a cross-border, US–Mexico collaboration with commentary by women who are not "easy to manage."

Maquilapolis presents the sweatshop reality that was the basis from which Alex Rivera's *Sleep Dealer* was a sci-fi (but nevertheless realistic) extrapolation. Whereas the sign at the edge of Tijuana where Memo enters reads "Tijuana: The World's Largest Border Town," in *Maquilapolis*, a sign is seen on a bridge above a highway that reads "Tijuana: The World Capital of Television."

Funari and De La Torre's film articulates a present that is a function of a "historical conjunction of contingent elements" among which are a "geographic border between Mexico and the United States, created by past wars, [and] the asymmetric development of the two economies."[45] It follows the lives of two women, Carmen Durán and Lourdes Luján, whose factory, in flagrant violation of labor laws, extracts "an hour of drudge work" for them to have earned enough to buy "a jug of potable water."[46] The spatial reality within which the documentary is situated is the 4,000 multinational-owned factories bunched near the US border, where a workforce comprised of a majority of women feels privileged to be earning as much as US$11 a day, given the extreme poverty and high unemployment in the region. While the theme of the film is familiar, focused as it is on the exhausting, morbidity-causing tempo and duration of the work (for example, Carmen worked the night shift assembling flybacks, parts in Sanyo television sets, in a factory whose milieu is so toxic that she ended up with serious kidney disease), the form of the documentary is unusual. Carmen and Lourdes are both objects of analysis and meaning-producing subjects. They are the film's collaborators and narrators.

Maquilapolis begins with a group of the women pantomiming the bodily rhythms demanded by the repetitive nature of their assembly-line work (Figures 4.4). It then proceeds to a reading of the work and local living experiences through the perspectives of Carmen and Lourdes, who function as both aesthetic and ethnographic subjects (in terms of the former, their bodies map the life-world within which they toil, while as the latter, their testimony and observations interpret that world). Their bodies as residents and workers dominate the documentary, which follows their movements and records their commentaries. In place of the abstract, macropolitical commentaries on the economic advantages of sweatshop employment are concrete effects of the factory work and the impact of the factory on the local environment. Both women deliver critical commentaries on the factory work and its milieu and end up as activists (*promotores*). Carmen, whose health has been seriously compromised by the working conditions in the Sanyo factory, heads a group of former employees whose case before the labor relations board wins them substantial severance pay. (Sanyo leaves for a cheaper labor market in Indonesia "with their pockets full and ours empty...They wanted to pay less and make more," as Carmen puts it.) And Lourdes heads a cooperative that manages to produce a cross-border initiative between US and Mexican environmental protection agencies to get a toxic waste site in their neighborhood (left over from a factory's abandoned plant) cleaned up.

Figure 4.4 Maquilapolis women pantomiming their work rhythms

Ultimately, like nineteenth-century economic commentaries, the film puts the working body at the center of
political economy, giving back to those bodies "the com-
plexities of their own determinations."[47] However, whereas
the nineteenth-century commentaries of Ricardo and
Malthus treated bodies only in terms of their endurance
or lack of same, the film gives them a speaking voice in a
way that accords with Jacques Rancière's perspective on
political "subjectification," "a series of actions of a body
and a capacity for enunciation not previously identifiable
within a given field of experience, whose identification is
thus part of the reconfiguration of the field of experience."[48] Carmen and Lourdes' acts of political subjectification are punctuated throughout the film by a gestural
chorus line of working women, whose voices are mute as
they mime the working rhythms that their factories have
imposed on them. Through those dramatic juxtapositions
(as well as through Carmen and Lourdes' commentaries
and political action), the film enacts an exemplary political
challenge to the degrading and debilitating choreography
of *maquiladora* factory work and to the factory's toxic
effects on the local environment.

Music and dance

There's a historical parallel between the commodification
of music and its appropriation within the hegemonic
cultural policies of Fordist industries. As Jacques Attali
famously points out, where once music was "a locus of
subversion," produced by people on the social margins –
for example, in the case of "Dionysian rites in Greece
and Rome, and…other cults (which were) at odds with
the official religions and centers of power"[49] – once it
entered the concert hall and thereafter hit broadcast
space and thus the realm of repeatability (through
recording technologies), it was transformed into a commodity and was appropriated "as a tool reinforcing rep-
resentative power."[50]

A similar musical trajectory is in evidence in the history of the factory. Before broadcast music was piped into factories with Fordist assembly lines in order to reinforce a rapid work rhythm, workers sang their own songs, which had intrinsic or personal value, "ensuring a singer personal resilience in the face of repetitive and burdensome forms of labour." The singing added an affective dimension that had the effect of "rallying their spirits."[51] However, as industrialization proceeded, there was a rapid decline in self-produced music as a result of the professional commercialization and rationalization of music's production and performance.[52] And workers' self-produced and sung music disappeared by the mid-twentieth century because factory owners (e.g., Henry Ford) wanted to cultivate *homo economicus*, a "degraded and deskilled" component of a rationalized assembly line rather than *homo faber*, a creative, self-motivated worker.[53]

While owners had silenced worker singing in the first half of the twentieth century, by the 1940s the music that returned to the factory was broadcast music: "workers were no longer the creators of their own music but were positioned as passive listeners hearing the music controlled by the employer. Significantly, a common kind of piped-in factory music came from the soundtracks of Busby Berkeley films in which a "mechanical chorus line 'joyfully affirmed the progress of rationalization.'"[54] As one analyst puts it, "employers and psychology researchers effectively created factory music as a 'twentieth-century technique for the control of the productive self.'"[55] The music was designed to aid and abet Fordist assembly line and Taylorist scientific management work styles by creating rhythms that encouraged rapid work choreographies; "familiar types of dance music, with their well-marked rhythms and distinctive melodies, were the most popular and effective stimulants to production and pleasure in work."[56] In England, the BBC broadcasts, under the rubric of *Music While You Work*, had a specific agenda for effective selections: "Please no slow foxtrots, tangos, waltzes, dreamy numbers of any sort, vocals of the sob-stuff order, complicated cross-rhythm in hot jazz numbers, selections with frequent changing style and speed, but plenty of snap and punch, rhythm of a straightforward kind, clean, clear-cut melody, brightness of all sorts."[57] Certainly, there was worker resistance "when they perceived that the music was being used to deliberately pace the work." For example, one worker complained, "There is one thing I cannot stand about the factory. That's the wireless. It's blaring jazz all day long...It's supposed to increase production and they say it has but it hasn't increased mine...it's driving me to distraction. I know there's several others like me."[58]

The "jazz," which is the source of complaint, is doubtless not the innovative call and response, open-ended versioning (emerging from a variety of Afro assemblages, e.g., Afro-Caribbean and African-American) that blurs the boundary between composing and playing but rather the white orchestral appropriation and commercialization of jazz, which "resulted in a music that was less improvisatory, less dependent on the inventiveness of soloists...and had led to a sameness of sound and style among the various bands."[59] The African-American non-closural versioning, which has been appropriately characterized as "willfully harsh, anti-assimilation,"[60] is ill suited to the kind of background music used in factories to promote a consistent and rapid work rhythm. The emphasis of the creative versions of blues and jazz music harks back to the pre-broadcast self-produced singing in factories; because in its African-American incarnation – e.g., in the composing/playing of Louis Armstrong – "the emphasis is on self-expression"[61] and in the creative versioning of John Coltrane, which "has special debts to the African American practice of playing with intelligibility." It is a constant testing of the boundaries of musical intelligibility rather than a mere playing of a set score.[62] And, crucially, as jazz developed as an African-American cultural and political practice, it was meant not only for listening but also for bodily resonance; it was supposed to provoke and accompany dance ("It Don't Mean a Thing [If It Ain't Got That Swing]," as Duke Ellington famously put it).

Not surprisingly, Henry Ford, the entrepreneur most responsible for inventing the docile working body amenable to the rapid rhythms of the assembly line, was notably hostile to jazz music. Like other elitist racists, he feared "the loss of white Anglo-Saxon hegemony in American political life and culture," and viewed jazz and jazz dancing as an anarchy-encouraging practice that undermined discipline. To counter jazz's growing popularity, he fostered the return of "old time" music, which was connected with a threatened, rural way of life by using his automobile dealerships to sponsor music and dance events, displacing jazz with "old-time fiddling" and jazz dancing with "old-time square and round dancing."[63] However, the primary music and dance supports for white hegemony have been choral songs and chorus-line dances – starkly illustrated for example in Rogers and Hammerstein's Broadway musical *Oklahoma!* in which the "songs and dance routines [are] addressed to a crucial stage in Euro American nation building...when Oklahoma experienced a rapid white in-migration and was about to change from territory to state...The choral song ['Many a New Day'...] celebrates the transition from territory to state," and "side-by-side [round] dance routines" [of white women] articulate "a movement from separate idiom to integrated genre, a movement toward an organic whole."[64]

Those same choral songs, along with chorus-line dancing, are important features of what Mark Franko designates as "Taylorized choreography," in which "the chorus girl exemplified the emotional equilibrium that Taylorist management sought in workers."[65] Exemplary is "the opening number of *Gold Diggers of 1933*"[66] – a chorus-line song and dance entitled "We're in the Money," in which (as Siegfried Kracauer puts it) "they joyfully affirmed the progress of rationalization,"[67] for "the dancing body" is aligned with "specialized tasks on the model of scientific management."[68] However, there were critical counter-dance initiatives as well in the 1930s. For example, challenging the Fordist/Taylorist-affirming chorus-line musicals was a radical modern dance genre "reacting to capitalism and racism."[69] Among these is Jane Dudley's *Time is Money* (1934) in which "an oppressed figure weaves in and out of a circle of light in center stage while a speaker outside the circle, looking in, recites a poem by Sol Funaroff about labor as suffering."[70] "The dancer's rhythms are repeatedly accelerated by work [and] Dudley says, 'There is one section where he starts to work and then gets feebler and feebler and collapses' [subsequently attempting] to physically articulate machine-like alacrity of arm and head with a collapsed and trembling frame, alternating energetic resolve with withered frailty."[71]

Ultimately, however, Dudley's dancer becomes politically subjectivated, breaking out of the circle of light.

> Now facing the public outside the circle of harsh work light, she appears strong and demanding but also newly self-contained. The entirety of her physical and emotional self-assumption comes into focus. No longer striving, she looks out, then down briefly at her own fists clenched at hip level, then again out at the audience, with an expression of both shock and awakening. Stopping to confront her audience, and bringing the dance to a halt, the dancer appropriates time as essential to the *performative* economy.[72]

Cinema Articulated with Dance: Lars Von Trier's *Dancer in the Dark*

There's a striking moment of subversion of the work rhythms in a metal-sink-making factory in Lars Von Trier's musical film *Dancer in the Dark* (2000). Combining cinema, music, and dance, that moment is an artistic critique that recalls the primary inspiration for this investigation, Fanon's injunction to resist a functionalist focus on output and the intensification of the rhythms of work. And it shows how dance operates as resistance to the ways factories have quarantined bodily rhythms, using them as vehicles for the production of value that ends up wholly external to the space of work. As Randy Martin has suggested, "dance might be taken as a key site where bodies in movement make value, and where circulation is fully inside of production in ways that yield insights into what sociality can be."[73] The scene that inaugurates the song and dance routine, "Cvalda," in Von Trier's film articulates such a spontaneous value-creating sociality. It opens with the camera on the film's main protagonist, Selma (Björk), as she works at her machine, accompanied by rhythmic sounds of hers and the other machines, which coordinate to articulate a syncopated rhythm that renders the factory as a music and dance hall. As the scene proceeds, the rhythms intensify to the point at which Selma's body has begun resonating to the factory's music. She breaks away from her machine and starts singing and dancing to the rhythms of the factory's sounds, while singing the song, "Cvalda." Selma's song and dance become contagious and other workers join her in dance steps while doing hand and arm gestures that mimic the choreography of their work at their machines (Figure 4.5). The scene is not unlike the opening and subsequent scenes in the

Figure 4.5 Cvalda, from *Dancer in the Dark*

above-analyzed documentary, *Maquilapolis*, in which the women workers perform *their* work choreography. However, while the women in *Maquilapolis* are configured as a chorus line, the workers in *Dancer in the Dark* undergo the kind of changing configurations that characterize dance choreographies in Broadway musicals.

As the dance and song rhythms take over, the factory space is deterritorialized as it changes from a zone of coerced rhythm to one of artistic expression and playful exuberance. The effect is in accord with the way Gilles Deleuze and Felix Guattari theorize the constitution of a new territory: "There is a territory precisely when milieu components cease to be directional, becoming dimensional instead, when they cease to be functional to become expressive."[74] Von Trier's camera work is well attuned to Deleuze and Guattari's observation. While the non-musical scenes in the film are captured with a single hand-held digital camera (which gives the non-musical moments of the film a documentary feel), Von Trier uses one hundred cameras to do this scene, shifting the space of the factory from its "directional" assembly choreography to a complex, multi-"dimensional" space of performance. The scene is filmed from many different angles and heights with camera work that is typical in film versions of Broadway musicals. And, unlike the documentary moments, those that mimic film versions of Broadway musicals are bright with strong color, distinguishing those fantasy moments as Selma's escape from the drudgery of the factory.

The film narrative is disjunctive with the musical moments. Briefly, Selma is a single mother who is losing her sight and is trying to earn enough money to get an operation for her son who, without it, is also destined to lose his sight. While the narrative as melodrama has Selma in a fraught relationship with a neighbor, Bill Houston (David Morse), who steals her money, has his death attributed to her as a murder, and ends in her execution, the film-as-musical has a different resonance. The musical moments are Selma's lines of flight. As she finds her voice, the film stages a critical encounter between sight and sound; Selma "sees through music,"[75] which, as she dances to it, transports her corporeally from one whose gestures are locked into the sounds of the factory to one who "self-produces" her music and gestures. At the same time, as a whole the film also stages an encounter between the rhythms of the rationalized and coercive choreography of the factory with the rhythms of the fantasy world of the musical show ("the world of the film musical begins where reality and the fantasy rhythmic world of the show merge"[76]).

Von Trier's very authentic recreation of the world of the musical is deceptive. He had "to turn up the colors in the dance sequences to make people feel that there were different levels of the film," not to simply copy the "standard Hollywood movie musical."[77] Although many of his musical scenes mimic the very Busby Berkeley musical films that ultimately lent soundtracks piped into the Fordist/Taylorist factory, Von Trier's musical moments effectively re-inflect the significance of those same song and dance routines as he creates a radical opposition between the world of the factory and the world of the musical. In his "fanciful gesture to the Hollywood aesthetic he normally eschews,"[78] Von Trier contrasts the reality of factory work with Selma's escapes to musical fantasies, filmed in a style that separates them from the factory world. In so doing, he invents an aesthetic subject who, as she opts out of the rationalized and oppressive rhythms of the world of work, shows us a counter-world of creative sonic and rhythmic exuberance. Ultimately, the politics of aesthetics articulated in Von Trier's *Dancer in the Dark* is a creative response to Fanon's call to resist the subjugation of the rhythms imposed by choreographies of capitalist work practices.

Dance Yet Again

While Von Trier's film shows a dance routine articulated as a brief moment of labor resistance to an imposed

Figure 4.6 Gumboot dancers

choreography, the resistance to which Fanon referred has yielded an enduring dance form in South Africa, the "gumboot dance." It's a form that emerged from the South African working class that labored in the mines of Witwaterstrand, South Africa. Forced to work in oppressive conditions – chained together, beaten, and abused, while standing in flooded mines – they were given rubber Wellington boots in lieu of having the water drained. Dealing with an enforced silence, the workers developed a dance form, using the gumboots as a mode of communication: "slapping their boots, stamping their feet, and rattling their ankle chains," while singing about their oppressive conditions. As "some employers eventually became aware of this emerging dance form…the more tolerant ones allowed the best dancers to form troupes" (see Figure 4.6). Although the mine owners used the performances to create public relations (PR) for their enterprises, "It was not unusual for these performers' songs, sung in the workers' native languages, to openly mock their bosses and criticize wages and conditions, while the bosses listened in, blissfully ignorant of the content."[79]

Conclusion: "The Corporate Sublime"/ "The Sweatshop Sublime"

The mine owner's appropriation of gumboot performance for purposes of PR is an instance of what Dominic Pettman

calls "the corporate sublime," moments when corporations "valorize the human element" to give the impression
that the commodity chain linking production with consumption is benign rather than exploitive. Drawing on
examples from the "visual rhetoric" in PR of Dow Chemical and Cisco Systems, Pettman asserts that "the corporate
sublime...weav[es] the micro and macro in such a way as
to suggest profound global connections between people of
all colors and creed," thereby interpolating the global
consumption assemblage, not by hailing them (chez
Althusser) in a commanding way, but in "a seductive and
inspiring one."[80]

Bruce Robbins, evoking an aspect of that sublime, the
"sweatshop sublime," ponders our inattention to the
oppressive conditions at the production end of the commodity chain, as he identifies a stark disjunction in our
desire for tracing the agency of products: "[I]n the case of
art...we actively desire to *remember* the human pro-
ducer...[I]f we want to see traces of production...[we]
will pay good money in order to have their voices in our
heads." He goes on to ask why we don't "want the same
thing with other products as well, products that are not
classified as art."[81] As an example of our inattention to the
conditions of production of the things we use, Robbins
provides this scenario:

> One morning, while getting dressed, you either do or do
> not examine the label of your shirt. If you do, you either
> do or do not realize the conditions of life under which this
> shirt was, or perhaps was not, produced: the pitifully inad-
> equate wages, not to speak of the locked fire exits, the
> arbitrary harassments and firings, the refusal of genuine
> union representation, and so on.[82]

Robbins evokes the Kantian sublime to supply a politically perspicuous conceptual frame for treating the kind
of attention that can unite our "small world" of product
use with the larger world, carrying our imagination to "the

outer reaches of a world economic system of notoriously inconceivable magnitude and interdependence, a system that brings goods from the ends of the earth...in order to satisfy your slightest desire." He points out that this hard-to-conceive larger world fits well within Immanuel Kant's "descriptions of the sublime...a feeling of inadequacy of [the] imagination for presenting the ideas of a whole, wherein the imagination reaches its maximum, and, in striving to surpass it, sinks back into itself, by which, however, a kind of emotional satisfaction is produced."[83] For Kant, the sublime evokes an "intellectual feeling" – for example, in response to a huge storm – but what evokes it "is not nature" per se "but rather magnitude, force, quantity in its purist state, a 'presence' that exceeds what imaginative thought can grasp at once in a form – what it can *form*."[84] Translated into Robbins's example: after imagining that difficult-to-conceive world of global production and product delivery, one returns from that challenge to the imagination to one's "everyday smallness."[85]

The main implication of Robbins's framing of our relationship with the products of sweatshop labor is the question of our responsibility: "I have been arguing against the sort of self-aggrandizing that often hides out in calls to activist responsibility...I've been trying to give a more modest and more accurate sense of what our responsibilities are, but not a less binding one."[86] As Robbins goes on to point out, the movement of "heavy industry," e.g., "from Manchester and Milwaukee to Mexico and Malaysia," creates complications and thus challenges for "seeing, speaking and acting trans-nationally," and suggests that it is "at this point that expertise in cognitive and aesthetic practice can properly claim to be of use, and even of significance."[87]

I want to highlight Robbins's phrase "aesthetic practice," and return briefly to Kant's analytic of the sublime, where Kant frets about the possibility of an effectively shared ethos. Given that Kant had placed his hopes for a global ethical *sensus communis* on a shared moral sense (which is articulated in his second critique, the *Critique of Practical Reason*), he found himself admitting that, in the case of the sublime, large forces (e.g., of nature) threaten our reliance on reason: "The feeling of the Sublime is...a feeling of pain, arising from a want of accordance between the aesthetical estimation of magnitude formed by the Imagination, and the estimation of the same formed by Reason."[88] As I have noted elsewhere, Kant assumed that the solution was to be found at the level of subjective consciousness, that "the dynamic of subjectivity would overcome the discordance among the faculties provoked by the sublime and result in a subjective attunement or necessity that would bode well for a politics of freedom."[89] Robbins, wisely I think, returns to Kant's "Analytic of the Beautiful" and suggests that Kant, rather than seeking to defend rationality, sees the possibility of a subjective necessity in people's "uncoerced and individual yet also universalizing act of appreciating the beautiful [not in] their rational obedience to the good."[90]

Here, I want to stick with the sublime, where we observe a less confident Kant and contrast Kant's hope for "accordance" in the face of discordance (based on a model of culture that contains a shared natural moral sensibility[91]) with the way Jacques Rancière derives "implications of the sublime for a politics of aesthetics," where he derives an "aesthetic of disagreement" rather than harmony from Kant's sublime and offers a politics that resists a model of consensus that "pins people down to their proper places" in order to highlight the disjuncture between "those who work and those whose leisure is won on the back of workers."[92] Robbins suggests that, at a minimum, "we" (academics with pretentions to political influence) must migrate out of our small world of privacy to connect with the larger world of labor exploitation: "if the public intellectual is to pursue something higher than publicity, this continuing communion with privacy [connecting our small world with the larger word of economic inter-dependence] is an inescapable part of her task."[93] I agree but want to note as well, based on the analysis I have offered of resistant initiatives by workers, that our attention to the world of privation associated with the commodity chain can be summoned by a politics of aesthetics, articulated in critically oriented documentary cinema. And I want to add that there is another genre that can also summon our attention, the artistic installation, which as Jaimey Hamilton Faris shows, belongs to recent histories of counter-commodity, counter-consumer specular strategies [with which] "contemporary readymade art tries to subvert, or at least ironize, commodity specular culture."[94] Among her examples is the art collective, subRosa, whose manifesto is to connect "the worker and the consumer," with a special emphasis on women's affective labor. They have created an installation that invites the visitor to connect their apparel with the production end of the consumption chain. The installation *Can You See Us Now?* (Figure 4.7) has "a large map with scissors tethered to it, inciting visitors to cut off all the tags on their clothing and pin them onto the map according to their 'made in' location, thus charting evidence of worldwide apparel commodity chains."[95]

Figure 4.7 The subRosa installation

Kant's "Analytic of the Sublime," which provides a frame to call our attention to how the local (small) world connects with the hard-to-conceive larger world of commodity production, is also serviceable as a frame for how our imagination, focused primarily on our everyday life-world, can be elevated to consider the larger world within which enmities are materially actualized, as unmanned weaponized drones implement those enmities, directed from local spaces where targeting decisions end up destroying bodies in remote spaces. To capture that reality, I refer to a "weapons sublime," a framing that illuminates a reverse (and deadly) commodity chain, produced locally and used/experienced remotely. In chapter 5, I turn to a variety of genres, documentary cinema among others, which call that "weapons sublime" to our attention.

5

"Fictions of Time": Necro-Biographies

Introduction: A Weapons Sublime

I ended chapter 4 with a focus on our inattention to the production end of the commodity chain: the problem of sustaining an imagination that connects our local, small world to the larger world of interdependence responsible for making available what we consume. Here, as I suggested at the end of chapter 4, I want to treat our inattention to another global interconnection, in this case a reversal of the direction of the commodity chain – something produced locally that impacts a larger world of vulnerable "consumers" (people abroad who are targeted by weapons launched from our domestic space). Recalling chapter 1's reference to how news of atrocities becomes old very quickly and to the genres that facilitate slow looking by bringing back those violent episodes in genres that create a space for reflection to give them renewed and altered significance, I want to revisit the media- and genre-atrocity issue, inspired in part by a section in Grégoire Chamayou's *A Theory of the Drone*. Chamayou refers to the deadly epistemology deployed in the selection of people for targeted assassinations, an epistemology, he asserts, that is derived from "The tools of human geography and the sociology of networks…[employed] to pick out dangerous individuals." He goes on to state:

> Officials claim that these methods ensure selective targeting: "you can track individuals and – patiently and carefully – build up a picture of how they move, where they go and what they see," noted a US counterterrorism official. Those who end up being killed "are those people whose actions over time have made it obvious that they are a threat."[1]

Alerted by this revelation of a series of murder-justifying biographical speculations which rapidly turn what is arbitrary into what is regarded as "obvious," in this chapter I locate those brief biographies of targeted individuals and groups – what I term *necro*-biographies – in the context of a history of partialities and interests through which biographies are assembled or produced. I then turn to genres that offer what I will call counter-biographies, based on alternative perspectives to the life stories that have rendered drone targets obvious. Because the brief bios of targeted victims rarely emerge outside of the archives created by the militarized gaze and apparatuses of implementation that order assassinations on the basis of the accreted "evidence," drone targeting atrocities against thousands of (mostly innocent) victims, whose deaths rarely rise above the threshold of recognition, receive little public attention. Accordingly, before exploring the genres that provide "counter-visions"[2] and counter-biographies, I want to explore the vagaries of attention.

Media Genres and Attention

What determines the level and persistence of attention to atrocities? What are the practices that conceal them? Certainly, diverse media – official government releases, journals, newspapers, television and internet publications, as well as what is treated by a variety of artistic genres – provide what people know about atrocities, starvation, and other forms of adversity all over the planet. And, crucially, each media genre has a different effect on the powers of attention. Unfortunately, the short attention span of journalistic media (noted in chapter 1), which abandons its coverage of episodes of violence and suffering after giving them brief exposure, is congenial with people's short attention spans for heeding adversity at both historical and geographic distances. To reflect on this latter aspect of inattention, I turn to a text I have analyzed in another investigation, Zadie Smith's story, "The Embassy of Cambodia," which features as the protagonist, Fatou, an Ivorian domestic servant in an Anglo-Indian household in a suburb of London, who passes by the Cambodian Embassy on her daily walks.[3]

The story treats in parallel the atrocities committed during the Khmer Rouge genocide of a large portion of the Cambodian population, decades ago, and the current atrocities experienced by migrant domestic workers from poor countries, working in the households of families residing in wealthy ones. In the case of Fatou, Smith's protagonist, there is no egregious brutality, although the wife and mother of the household, Mrs Derawal, "had twice slapped her in the face, and the two older children spoke to her with no respect at all and thanked her for nothing. (Sometimes she heard her name used as a term of abuse between them. 'You're as black as Fatou' or 'You're as stupid as Fatou')."[4] For my purposes here, I focus on the way the story articulates the problem of attention through the reflections of both the narrator and Fatou. Explaining why the people of Willesden feel uneasy about having the Cambodian Embassy in their suburb while failing to engage in lengthy reflection about the violent episode for which the embassy is a material reminder, the narrator says, "We [the residents of Willesden] were surprised by the appearance of the Embassy of Cambodia...It is not the right sort of surprise, somehow. [However]...the fact is if we followed the history of every little country in this world...we would have no space left in which to live our own lives or to apply ourselves to necessary tasks."[5] As I have noted elsewhere, "The story implies that the hiddenness of war crimes and atrocities is owed as much to the psychic suppressions of the phenomenology of everyday life as it is to suppression strategies of government-controlled media."[6]

The phenomenology of inattention to forms of distant adversity is also addressed explicitly by Fatou, whose abuse by the Derawals provokes her reflections on her condition, once she begins to connect the Embassy-as-historical-symbol to her position (as well as to indentured domestic servants in the United Kingdom in general). She is also alerted by a media encounter; she sees, "in a discarded *Metro* found on the floor of the Derawal kitchen...a story about a Sudanese 'slave' living in a rich man's house in London...It was not the first time that Fatou had wondered if she herself was a slave." That pondering migrates into her thoughts about a history of atrocities outside the boundaries of the United Kingdom – various historical mass killings. For example, thinking about the Cambodian extermination campaign, she says to her Nigerian friend Andrew Okonkwo (employed as a night guard) that "more people died in Rwanda...And nobody speaks about that! Nobody."[7] However, she is subject to the same pressure for inattention as the citizens of Willesden. When Fatou refers in the same conversation to Rwandan atrocities about which "nobody speaks," Andrew rejoins with mention of the Hiroshima atomic bombing. Fatou then realizes "that she had heard the story before...But she felt the same vague impatience with it as she did with all accounts of suffering in the distant past, for what could be done about the suffering of the past?"[8]

The impatience displayed by Smith's Fatou in the face of the welter of information about atrocities is subject to an incisive reflection by Imre Kertész (the Hungarian novelist referenced in the Preface and in chapter 2) on what can best be conceived as the atrocity sublime. Kertész invents protagonists who mirror much of his experience as a Holocaust survivor (he spent more than three of his teenage years in concentration camps). In his second novel devoted to that experience, *Fiasco*, there is a moment in which his protagonist is trying to absorb the facts associated with Nazi atrocities. He complains that "the problem with facts, however important they may otherwise be, is that there are too many of them and they rapidly wear fantasy down."[9] As he is trying to sort the many facts, he comes across a report about "the deaths of 340 Dutch Jews at a stone quarry [in the concentration camp] Mauthausen," many of whom leaped to their deaths while being forced to carry impossibly huge boulders uphill. In response, the narrator says that in the face of those and other horrible facts, "Rather than becoming a plaything, the imagination proves to be a heavy and immovable burden, just like those boulders in Mauthausen: people do not want to be crushed under them... [As a result] [w]e live our lives without being enriched by the experiences of our era."[10] Despite how overwhelming the effect of horrible facts may be on one's imagination, Kertész's writing (his acts of imagination) constitutes a form of political agency, in his case the articulation of a "truth" on behalf of "the dead," which he insists belong to them and "no one else."[11]

Similarly, through the creation of a fictional biography, Smith's story performs agency, a form of critical attention as it dramatizes atrocities that tend to fade from historical memory. Although Smith dwells to some extent on Fatou's victimization, with the effect of disclosing a shadow world of abuse that rarely achieves public visibility, at the same time she lends Fatou a form of agency. In her story, the political subjectification of her protagonist derives from the imagery and compositional structure of the writing. Fatou's political activism is implied through the story's narrative of what Fatou observes. The Cambodian Embassy, which is described as a less-than-grand edifice ("It is only a four- or five-bedroom North London suburban villa") is "surrounded by a red brick wall, about eight feet high,"[12] which Fatou often passes on her way to swim at a private club." As her access to the embassy is limited to what she can see and hear from the outside, she becomes aware of a badminton game continually under- way behind the wall as she passes it each day. She sees a shuttlecock arcing "back and forth, cresting this wall hori- zontally," and hears the hits, "Pock, smash. Pock, smash,"[13] doubtless sounds that make her think about the beatings involved in the Khmer Rouge torture scenarios.

The arcing shuttlecock and the onomatopoeias serve in the story as "encountered signs," which, as Gilles Deleuze suggests, are the conditions of possibility for thinking, learning, and (in many cases) acting. Applying the concept in his study of Proust, Deleuze refers to the kind of worldly signs that evoke such instances of spatio-temporal distance that Fatou experiences with respect to the Khmer Rouge atrocities: "Doubtless the 'world' expresses social, histori- cal and political forces. But the worldly signs are emitted in a void. Thereby they traverse astronomic distances, so that observation of worldliness bears no resemblance to study by microscope, but rather to study by telescope."[14]

Crucially, from a Deleuzian perspective, for Fatou to be affected enough to think politically, the embassy must not be a mere object of recognition, or

> a representation of something already in place [because w] ith such a non-encounter our habitual way of being and acting in the world is reaffirmed and reinforced, and as a consequence no thought takes place. [In contrast]…with a genuine encounter…our typical ways of being in the world are challenged, our systems of knowledge disrupted [so that] we are forced to thought.[15]

Heeding Drone-Killing Atrocities

Inasmuch as what is available to the average US media consumer – major network news whose coverage controls

both the visual frame and the discourses within which
most people experience US policy – thought-provoking
challenges to official images and languages of counterterrorism are not widely disseminated. Few media consumers
become aware of the on-the-ground consequences of US
drone strikes around the world, which murder scores of
innocent non-combatants. As a result (and not surprisingly) by recent estimates, only 13 percent of the US population has a negative attitude to drone-targeted killings. As
I've suggested, much of the reason for the relative absence
of policy critique available to the general public is the
tendency of mainstream media to recycle the rationales for
targeted killing by reporting rather than questioning official statements about who has been killed. Marjorie Cohen
summarizes the official perspective unblinkingly:

> On "Terror Tuesdays," [President Barack] Obama and
> John Brennan, Obama's former counterterrorism advisor,
> now CIA director, go through the "kill list" to identify
> which individuals should be assassinated that week. The
> Obama administration has developed a creative method to
> count the civilian casualties from these assassinations. All
> military-age men killed in a drone strike are considered to
> be combatants...Brennan falsely claimed in 2011 that no
> civilians had been killed in drone strikes in nearly a year.[16]

To challenge that perspective, accepted by a suborned
mainstream media, I heed Deleuze's suggestion about
critical encounters and turn to two artistic genres that
challenge rather than affirm what Deleuze refers to as
"our habitual way of being and acting in the world" by
providing realistic encounters with (deadly) events that
must force us to think (and evince both sympathy and
outrage). One is the Showtime television series *Homeland*,
and the other is a documentary, *Unmanned: America's
Drone Wars*.

    Turning first to the former: the first episode in Season
Four of *Homeland* (2014), "The Drone Queen," provides

a realistic picture (based on actual events) of the precariousness of civilian non-combatants created by the US
"war on terror," as well as what is at stake for the careers
of those in the decision-making hierarchy when non-
combatants are targeted. As the episode begins, the station
chief in Kabul, Carrie Mathison (Claire Danes), recently
promoted to that position, gets a call from Sandy Bachman
(Corey Stoll), her Islamabad counterpart, that a "high-
value target," a leading Taliban insurgent, has been seen
in the tribal area of Pakistan. Being assured that the "intel"
is solid, she directs a couple of F-15 fighter jets to bomb
the target. As Carrie, her colleagues in the control room,
and the viewers are watching through the feed of a drone,
the targeted building is destroyed. Shortly thereafter, the
"intel" turns out to have been flawed. Carrie and her staff
learn from a news report that she has called in bombs on
a wedding party and killed 40 civilians (a fictional drama
reprise of an actual event).

When they send the drone back to give them a view of
the site of the bombing, they see a lone survivor, a young
medical student, Aayan Ibrahim (Suraj Sharma), looking
up at the drone, returning their gaze (Figure 5.1). After
they fret about who he might be, and the implications of
his having witnessed the atrocity, things get worse. His
smartphone camera has footage of the wedding party,
which goes viral when Aayan's politically zealous room-
mate sends the footage (which includes the bride and
little girls dancing) to YouTube. To make matters even
more precarious for the "drone queen" and the violence-
delivering security apparatus (*dispositif*) within which she
works, Sandy, who sent the "intel," is grabbed from a car
he's riding in with Carrie and her assistant, the Black Ops
specialist, Peter Quinn (Rupert Friend). Having been identified by an angry mob (informed and choreographed by
undercover personnel from Pakistan's intelligence service
(ISI)) seeking revenge for the atrocity, he's kicked to death
by the mob. Quinn prevents Carrie from trying to inter-
vene and drives away so that they can escape a similar fate.

Figure 5.1 Aayan returning the gaze

The consequences of the rash decision to blow up a building with civilians, and the inability to save Sandy, shakes
up the extended security apparatus (*dispositif*) within
which "anti-terrorist" weapons function.

As I have noted elsewhere, "a weapon, aside from its
operation as part of the killing operations of a fighting
force, is a complex design and commodity that emerges
from extensive interactions among political, commercial
and knowledge agencies, all involved in the larger (media-
propagated) motivations associated with global structures
of enmity and national structures of career advancement
and prestige."[17] After the bombing fiasco, it becomes
evident that there is a crucial temporality structuring the
weapons *dispositif*, taking it beyond its emergence to the
vagaries of its use. Those who are part of the decision
process through which the weapons are used are always
already in the future, justifying their targeting decisions.
An appreciation of that aspect of decision complexes was
rendered effectively in the methodological investigations
of Harold Garfinkel. In the inquiries in his *Studies
in Ethnomethodology*, Garfinkel's ethnographic subjects

(e.g., jurors deciding guilt or innocence and bureaucrats classifying suicides) are always already in a future scene of justification. In his words, "Decisions [have] an unavoidable futurity."[18]

In the *Homeland* episode, the presence of the witness, Aayan, bears on the CIA personnel's "futurity." What he has seen is threatening to their careers, and in some cases the sheer survival of people at all levels of the US security apparatus, as well as those in oppositional apparatuses (Pakistan's ISI and the Taliban insurgent structure). Aayan is attacked and threatened by hired thugs from the ISI who warn him to no longer speak about the incident (he had been cornered and interviewed on television); he's taken in by Carrie and lured into sexual intimacy so she can extract information about the CIA's target, Aayan's uncle, Haissam Haqqani (Numan Acar), who turns out to be still alive; and when he goes into the mountains to bring medicine to his uncle, his uncle kisses his cheek and then shoots him because the drone circling overhead is there because Aayan has led it there, having been gulled into admitting that his uncle is alive. As it turns out, Aayan's return of the gaze incites all the relevant apparatuses to respond, giving us a view of all the networks (both friendly and hostile) involved in the post-9/11 "war on terror," articulated especially as what sociologists have deemed "moral careers."

Added to the complex agencies surrounding the incident is the situation of Saul Berenson (Mandy Patinkin), the former station chief who now works for a private security firm. While helping Carrie, he's abducted by ISI agents and turned over to Haqqani, where he effectively serves as a human shield. Although Carrie wants to "take the shot" from the drone to eliminate Haqqani, Quinn intervenes and prevents it because Saul would perish as well. Inasmuch as it has been well publicized that Saul, the former agency head, is a captive, the entire security *dispositif* is roiled. Added to the mistaken destruction of civilians is the inability of "the Company" to protect its staff. To theorize the pregnant implications for US security practices

that the episode provides, I turn to Jacques Lacan's treatment of the "gaze," which articulates the kind of trauma
experienced by members of the security apparatus in the
Homeland episode.

The Eye and the Gaze

In his lectures *The Four Fundamental Concepts of Psycho-
Analysis*, Jacques Lacan famously distinguishes the eye
and the gaze, where the latter involves a trauma-inducing
sense of being seen that disrupts the scopic field, undermin-
ing the viewer's confidence in being in control of her/his
perceptions. The gaze, he says, is "that which performs
like a phantom force...In our relation to things, in so
far as this relation is constituted by the way of vision,
and ordered in the figures of representation, something
slips, passes, is transmitted, from stage to stage, and is
always to some degree eluded in it – that is what we
call the gaze."[19]

Lacan's story about the emergence of his idea of the gaze
as psychically disruptive is as follows:

> I was in my early twenties...and at the time, of course,
> being a young intellectual, I wanted desperately to get
> away, see something different, throw myself into some-
> thing practical...One day, I was on a small boat with a
> few people from a family of fishermen...as we were
> waiting for the moment to pull in the nets, an individual
> known as Petit-Jean...pointed out to me something float-
> ing on the surface of the waves. It was a small can, a
> sardine can...It glittered in the sun. And Petit-Jean said to
> me – You see that can? Do you see it? Well it doesn't
> see you.[20]

Reflecting on the potential return of the gaze suggested
by Petit-Jean's remarks, Lacan saw the returned gazed as
yet another aspect of the way subjects are alienated from
themselves, in this case by their decentered placement in

the field of vision, where they experience themselves as objects of the gaze of others. The trauma they experience is the result of a returned gaze that does not coincide with the place from which they see the world.[21] It becomes evident that they do not control the scopic field. In the case of the *Homeland* episode, the lack of control has high stakes for the security collective ranging from the White House to the fields of operation and from targeting rationales developed by the nation's primary decision makers to those who implement them.

From the Drone Queen to the Drone *Dispositif*

Although *Homeland*'s Aayan is an aesthetic subject operating in a fictional story, the collective trauma effects of his return of the militarized, security-oriented gaze serves as a stand-in for much of the blowback that the United States' drone warfare has experienced. Among the functional equivalents of the return of the gaze is the Stanford-NYU investigation of the use of drones in Pakistan (noted in chapter 2), which summarizes the official position as follows: "In the United States, the dominant narrative about the use in Pakistan is of a surgically precise and effective tool that makes the US safer by enabling 'targeted killing' of terrorists with minimal downsides or collateral impacts."[22]

Countering that dominant narrative, the investigation (as I noted in chapter 2) disclosed an alarming level of atrocity visited on innocent civilians; "From June 2004 through mid-September 2012, available data indicate that drone strikes killed 2,562–3,325 people in Pakistan, of whom 474–881 were civilians, including 176 children."[23] Those disclosures, imitated effectively in Showtime's *Homeland*, bid to affect political and bureaucratic careers (the primary concern expressed by the fictional CIA head in *Homeland*, Andrew Lockhart (Tracy Letts). The precarity for him and the rest of the anti-terrorist drone warfare apparatus was played out in the hearings for the appointment of William Brennan, Obama's "drone warrior" as CIA director.[24] There, as before, he has been called to account as civilian deaths had mounted in both Pakistan and Yemen. Moreover, others who serve on the periphery of the drone *dispositif* have been questioned about their role in the thanato-political decision process that determines who gets targeted by the drones.

At the outset of the executive-level decision process, the selected targets were "militants" who were marked for assassination (extra-judicial killing) by a decision-making chain that frequently ran all the way up to the "commander-in-chief" and White House staff. The identity of the "militant" blurs the boundary (which historically is always already blurred) between combatants and non-combatants, while at the same time making the ethics or morality of war an issue that various media have begun raising anew.[25] Among other things, the roles of peripheral knowledge agents have become increasingly evident. For example, the targeting "intelligence" has been aided and abetted by a CIA security-oriented anthropology as the warrants for killing have turned from "personality" targeting to "signature" targeting (where the latter strikes are against "men believed to be militants associated with terrorist groups, but whose identities aren't always known."[26]

To repeat what I noted in chapter 2, the cultural "knowledge" solicited by the CIA has come from a suborned social science that has been recruited and/or has recruited itself into the security *dispositif*. The military and security agency designation for the cultural aspects of war zones is the "human terrain system." That "system's" representatives have been recruiting knowledge agents at meetings of the American Anthropological Association.[27] Strongly criticized by that Association, undeterred uniformed anthropologists have been embedded in both combat and intelligence operations. As Marshall Sahlins puts it, "The principal role of academics in the service of counterinsurgency is to develop the human intelligence (HUMANINT) that will allow a triage between those elements of the population to be attacked (or assassinated) and those it would be better not to – in brief, sophisticated targeting."[28]

Grégoire Chamayou raises a relevant question, "What authorizes someone to engage in manhunting?"[29] As I have suggested, the "what" is a complex set of interacting agencies and legitimations in which justifications and careers are colliding. And as regards the ethics of violence, there has been a step toward anonymous killing through a process in which the killers and those who authorize them (knowledge agents, intelligence agencies, and weapons operators) are epistemologically, physically, and perceptually remote. Prior to the advent of such remote killing, "a soldier's right to kill his or her opponents depend[ed] on the condition of mutual risk [so that those] piloting weaponized drones from the other side of the globe [are engaged in] riskless war … [thus creating a] deep challenge [to what has been called "the *morality* of warfare."[30] In addition to the ambiguity of what a riskless "warrior" flying a drone from a remote location can see is the change in the temporal structure of the targeting decision. The possible interval for sensitivity to civilian casualties (and mistaken "signatures") has been radically altered. In the case of drones, "the sensor (formerly the UAV [non-weaponized drone]) and the shooter (formerly a manned airplane, an artillery unit, etc.) no longer have to be coordinated but are now two-in-one, unmanned combat air vehicles (UCAVs) [that] reduce the sensor-to-shooter gap from hours to minutes or seconds."[31]

Although the temporality of the executions is sudden, the process through which the targets become eligible for execution has a slower pace. It's based, as I have suggested, on CIA anthropology, which in the period in which personality strikes have been supplemented with signature strikes (where the latter require a mapping of the relationship of people's locations and habitual movements to their likelihood of becoming dangerous) becomes the basis for necro-biographies. In order to challenge the epistemological support rendered to targeting by professional anthropologists (among others) and treat what I will call the return of the anthropological gaze, I want to rehearse an earlier such challenge I have addressed. As I noted in my treatment of war crimes:

> The primary discursive condition of possibility for the Nuremberg war crimes trials was a new collective subject, "humanity." Inasmuch as the Nazi death apparatuses included extensive anthropological concepts, which constituted hierarchical versions of human nature (for example, Alfred Hoche's notorious gloss on "life unworthy of life"), a juridical response required a counter anthropology as part of the Nuremberg justice dispositif. For that, "the conceptual development of a notion of 'crimes against humanity'" was crucial, even though that new collective subject, "humanity as a whole," as an object of a crime [fits] uneasily within established legal discourse.[32]

Recently, a counter-anthropology has been asserted against the anthropological supports of the droning *dispositif*. It is articulated in the second challenging genre I've noted, Robert Greenwald's documentary *Unmanned: America's Drone War*, which provides a powerful, evidence- and concept-heavy challenge to the United States' drone decision process. Along with the testimony of many who knew the victims of drone targeting is a sequence on an important cultural practice. The documentary shows a Jirga assemblage, a peaceful meeting in which cultural conflicts are mediated in Pakistan. The Jirga was attacked by hellfire missiles, shot from a drone, killing most of those assembled. While anonymous US officials are quoted to the effect that the assemblage was a terror-planning meeting (it wasn't the planning of a "bake sale," according to one), the documentary goes into the details of some of the members of the Jirga, providing information from cultural authorities about what was taking place and on the bios of those killed (supplied by family members).

As has been the case for many aspects of the abuses involved in the United States' "war on terror," documentary film, such as Greenwald's (which I treat more extensively below), continues to return the official gaze with artistic texts that (in Deleuze's terms) counter-actualize the events that have terrorized populations in (among other places) Pakistan and Yemen. The documentary genre-as-critique responds to the official "truth weapons" that Foucault has elaborated: posing the question, "What is the principle that explains history [and right]?", Foucault's answer is that it is to be found in "a series of brute facts" such as "physical strength, force, energy," in short, in "a series of accidents, or at least contingencies." However, governments "dissimulate the events of global violence by interpolating the use of raw force into the implementation of rationality and right."[33] In a passage that captures the sense of how the two governments use their truth weapon, he adds, "The rationality of calculations, strategies and ruses; the rationality of technical procedures that are used to perpetuate the victory, to silence...the war...[and he adds that] given that the relationship of dominance works to their advantage, it is certainly not in their [the government's] interest to call any of this into question." The counter to the truth weapon is "critique...the movement by which the subject gives himself the right to question truth on its effects of power and question power on its discourses of truth."[34]

Biographies and Counter-Biographies

Among the "truth weapons" that legitimate drone targeting is what Grégoire Chamayou refers to as a "necro-ethics" – a designation of the drone as "the humanitarian weapon par excellence" – articulated to support "the right to 'targeted assassination.'"[35] Here, I want to inflect that legitimation to treat the temporality of that targeting, which articulates itself as necro-biographies. As Chamayou points out, the anti-terrorist manhunts follow a "principle of creating an archive or film of everyone's life" (a brief biopic!) because, as he notes, "Optical surveillance is not limited to the present time. It also assumes the important function of recording and archiving." As a director of the surveillance contractor Logos Technologies puts it, "The idea behind persistent surveillance is to make a movie of a city-size area, with the goal of tracking all the moving vehicles and people."[36] "To locate [the] anonymous militants [whom they assassinate], targeters 'rely on what officials describe as "pattern of life analysis," using evidence collected by surveillance cameras on the unmanned aircraft and from other sources about individuals and locations [which they use] to target suspected militants, even when their full identities are not known.'"[37] The rigidity of the "pattern of life analysis," assembled from surveillance cameras with no nuanced ability to sort contexts, yields an inference that amounts to a "*dogmatism of appearances* not far removed from autism" (to borrow a phrase from Paul Virilio).[38]

Once the necro-biographies are produced, "those who end up being killed," says a US counterterrorism official, " 'are people whose actions over time have made it obvious that they are a threat.'"[39] Of course, biographies always have to be understood in the context of the ontologies and practices for interpreting and managing lives that are contemporaneous with their production. A securitized gaze, shaping the contemporary "war on terror" and the *dispositif* it has spawned provides the context for the necro-biographies which legitimate extra-judicial killing. A challenge to those necro-biographies therefore requires a critique of the presumed objectivity on which they are based – in the form of a counter-vision.

To prepare that challenge, I want to emphasize that the history of biography is among other things a history of the ontologies within which "life" has been understood and consequently a history of the loci of power over life. Without going into a lengthy chronology of the ontological- and power-invested frames within which lives have been interpreted, for purposes of illustration I jump first into medieval culture in which "the individual was seen as a symbol of the general"[40] and biographical writing, practiced as a didactic representation of exemplary lives, served to affirm the truth of the ontologies and the legitimacy of the power structures of theocratic societies involved in the "spiritual appropriations of reality"[41] (although the spiritual hegemony of those societies was often contested – for example by "Menocchio," a sixteenth-century Italian miller with a heterodox cosmology, whose biography stands as a challenge to the coercive practices that accompanied the Catholic church's cosmology).[42]

If we leap ahead a few centuries and land in the middle of the nineteenth, we discover a juridical biographical practice – another historical episode of the will to truth – described by Foucault in his gloss on the problem of the "dangerous individual in nineteenth-century legal psychiatry" (briefly reviewed in chapter 1).[43] Foucault refers to "the gradual emergence in the course of the nineteenth century of [an] additional character, 'the criminal'." Whereas in previous centuries, there were merely crimes and penalties, the nineteenth century witnessed the emergence of a new subject, which, having become an object of knowledge, was to be professionally interrogated and asked to provide an account (in effect, a brief autobiography) of her/his thoughts and impulses. As a result, conversations about the criminal/subject began taking place between doctors and jurists. Psychiatry had entered the courtroom because it was part of a new medical *dispositif*, concerned with "a sort of public hygiene" applied to a new target of governance, the social order. The brief bios extracted in courtrooms served a developing practice of governance, and the subjects of the bios were unable to provide much by way of counter-versions of their lives. However, while nineteenth-century defendants had little control over the interrogation of who they were, contemporary defendants – at least those with resources to hire a high-priced defense team – are better positioned to respond with counter-biographies, owed especially to video technologies. "Lawyers are beginning to submit biographical videos at sentencings." As one lawyer involved in creating a video for his client puts it, "Judges never knew the totality of the defendant before seeing these videos... All they knew was the case file."[44]

The modern courtroom is of course a mere annex of the contemporary governmentality within which governance, as Foucault points out, turned from a focus on the continuous reactivation of sovereign power – the power "to take life or let live" – to biopower, the management of life, which involves the power "to 'make' live or 'let' die."[45] Because the health and wellbeing of a new collective entity, the population, had become a focus of governance, the subjects of governance had become objects of knowledge rather than merely targets of procedures to ensure obedience. The development of public hygiene was among other things a concern with recruiting useful bodies, those able to serve in citizen armies, a concern that produced correlative calculating agencies. Accordingly, a medicine directed by the state is a medicine of cases. The gaze of the physician, no longer a healer, is deflected from the individual to the collective, and the health *dispositif* becomes radically entangled with the security *dispositif*.

Like Chamayou's critique of the epistemological assists to the security gaze (knowledge practices involved in creating the "terrorist," who is selected as a drone target), Foucault's brief account of the courtroom episode constitutes a political challenge to the epistemology of the medical gaze as it is deployed by knowledge agents who collaborate to create the "criminal" as a form of life. Would that there was a devil's advocate, someone providing a counter-bio on "Terror Tuesdays," to challenge the CIA necro-biographies in the face of which the targets have no "day in court." Be that as it may, both critiques

raise issues of the accountability of the biographical practices that constitute their respective subjects as objects of
knowledge designed to manage the threats of terrorism
and crime respectively. As I have noted elsewhere, biographies always serve some kind of interest: "All biography
has an ethical or valuational component, for there is no
neutral way to script a life [given that] there is no unmedi-
ated form of truth against which to judge biographical
truth. [As a result] the interesting question becomes one
of how biographies function."[46] Here, I want to supple-
ment that assertion by adding that what is also interesting
– indeed crucial – is the exposure of the biography to
accountability.

Biography and the Problem of Truth

The writing practices of diverse genres of biography have
operated within different truth regimes. One I want to note
briefly, a relatively benign epistemologically oriented way
of representing lives, belongs to a social science practice
known as psychobiography. Its knowledge emphasis, noted
in an investigation of "life histories and psychobiography,"
articulates what I have called an "ecumenical empiricism."[47] It is based on a representational model of truth,
evident in its assumption that a reliable version of a life,
"an optimal biography," can be achieved by weaving
together several different biographies of the same person.
But how can one decide what is central to a particular life,
and, as a result, what are the appropriate criteria to vali-
date the scripting of that life? Inevitably, every selection is
interest-based. The ecumenical empiricism I noted fails to
"appreciate that biographers are writers who participate in
[contentious] representational practices"[48] that render lives
useful to some form of authority or knowledge practice –
political, psychological, ethnographic, scientific, and so on.
    Sigmund Freud was keenly aware of the contentious
terrain within which biographical truth functioned. For

example, in his psychoanalytic biography of Leonardo da Vinci, he takes on the interpretive task of explaining "not only Leonardo's extraordinary achievements but also his general work style (his tendency to leave works unfinished) and some of the specific details on his work (Mona Lisa's smile in *La Giaconda* and why Mary's mother, St Anne, appears as youthful as she does."[49] Because the purpose of "his Leonardo study is to help vindicate psychoanalysis as a scientific, truth delivering discipline,"[50] his account is rife with epistemological codes and is delivered in a writing style that militates on behalf of objectivity; he mobilizes a grammar in which many of his sentences make psycho-analysis the active agent/author of his investigation, for example, "Let us lend an unprejudiced ear for a while to the psychoanalytic work, which, after all, has not yet spoken the last words."[51] In short, Freud was seeking to enhance the truth-value of his science; he was showing the analytic power of *his* version of psychoanalysis *vis-à-vis* competing versions (e.g., those of Jung and Adler) to account for the way Leonardo's psycho-sexual history articulated itself on his canvas.

To explore the biography–truth problematic further in an even more contentious conceptual terrain, I turn to another genre of biographical writing, the lives of political officials, and examine the controversy surrounding a presidential biography, Edmund Morris's *Dutch: A Memoir of Ronald Reagan*, in which the author invents himself as a witness to aspects of Reagan's life.[52] Morris's biography provides an exemplary case of the issue of biographical truth-value because his Reagan biography blurs the boundary between fiction and non-fiction. As Mark Maslan points out, Morris approached the biography as a witness, rather than as a reporter, in order to "close the historical gap between the subject and author." To do so, he had to augment "history with fiction."[53] Although Morris was widely condemned by historians and journalists for his "relativist approach to truth" (the book is more like "time-travel fiction than a conventional presidential biography"),[54] a good case can be made that what Morris did is more realistic than what he could have achieved with a conventional journalist-style report. That case can be made for cinema as well. For example, as Alain Resnais and Marguerite Duras presumed in constructing their response to the Hiroshima bombing in their *Hiroshima Mon Amour* as fiction rather than documentary (as Cathy Caruth infers), "direct archival footage cannot maintain the specificity of the event...that it is through the fictional story, not *about* Hiroshima but taking place at its site, that Resnais and Duras believe such historical specificity is conveyed."[55]

Jacques Rancière effectively makes the case for the reality effect in fiction, pointing out that a fictional component is inevitably involved, even when the text is not intended to be (in his terms) "avowed" as fiction. "Fiction," he suggests, "is a structure of rationality which is required wherever a sense of reality must be produced." Given that the truth problem is one of reality, not whether the text is avowed or unavowed, "[t]he point is not whether the description is true or false...the point is about the sense of reality produced by the cutting out of the scene, the identification of its elements and the modality of the description."[56] Elaborating, he writes:

> Literary fiction – or avowed fiction in general – is not so much the object that social science has to analyze as it is the laboratory where fictional forms are experimented as such and which, for that reason, helps us understand the functioning of form of unavowed fiction at work in politics, social science, or other theoretical discourses. It does so because it is obliged to construct what is at the heart of any fictional rationality but easily can be presupposed in the form of unavowed fiction: time, which means the form of coexistence of facts that defines a situation and the mode of connection between events that defines a story.[57]

Ultimately, there are two forms of time always involved, even in unavowed fiction: "the time of description which puts things beside one another like in a genre picture or a still life, and the time of action in which active characters interact with the movement of the social process."[58] Insofar as the fictional component of a text can be held to account, it is in terms of whether it is good or bad fiction, according to Rancière, where the good versus bad is based on the way time is treated. Good realist fiction recognizes the pervasive "conflict of temporalities which is a conflict between forms of life."[59] Thus, although Morris invented a character whose voice vehiculates the narrative of his Reagan biography, the facts he assembles, like any facts he might have put together without inventing a fictional narrator, would have had to rely on temporalities that are always fictional.

Thus Morris juxtaposes the temporality of Reagan's actual presence at events and places and Reagan's (faulty) memory of events and places. Through his invented presence, Morris witnesses Reagan's acts of imagination, and through his self-invention he stages an encounter between two fabulists. His invented presence in the past mediates the gap between the two persistent Reagan modes – what Reagan actually did and where he actually was, versus when and where Reagan imagined himself to be. As Morris puts it, "by making a literature out of Ronald Reagan," he wrote a realistic biography because he was able to convey how "Reagan lived in his own imagination."[60] Moreover, Morris's avowedly fictional approach to Reagan's biography is especially this apropos of the character. It comports well with "Reagan's own remarkable forays into biographical revisionism," as Michael Rogin has famously suggested. Ronald Reagan's life is best thought of as a fictional film, for "Reagan himself found out who he was through the roles he played on film [he]...merged his on- and off-screen identities"[61]; he manifested "an uncanny slippage between life and film."[62]

Most significantly for my purposes, the Reagan biography is in the public domain. Whatever challenges there have been to Morris's inventions, the text is entirely accessible, making Morris accountable for his inventions and insights about Reagan's life. What is at stake in the contention over the biography is the legacy of a presidency. The biography-as-event has produced no loss of life, only a potential discrediting of a life that in many versions is positively imagined (for example, a perspective visited by multitudes daily as they land and take off from Washington DC's "Reagan Airport").

CIA Fictions: "Terrorist" Biographies

To the extent that it will be continually heeded, Morris's Reagan biography bears on the future of the Reagan presidency, its ongoing will-have-been. The result of the CIA's "terrorist" biographies is to ensure the absence of a future for those targeted. The end of the victims' life trajectories is preceded by another temporality that Chamayou details. It's a process through which the "terrorist's" habitus is surveilled – his movements tracked, with the help of

> The tools of human geography and the sociology of social networks... enlisted in the service of a policy of eradication in which "persistent surveillance" makes it possible to pick out [the new] *dangerous individuals* [my emphasis]. The painstaking work of establishing an archive of lives progressively gathers together the elements of a file that, once it becomes thick enough, will constitute a death warrant.[63]

Thus, as I've suggested, the contemporary security state has re-inflected biopower. It now makes die rather than lets live, and to do so it mobilizes a thanatopolitical *dispositif* composed of political leaders and intelligence agency leaders, bureaucratic functionaries, knowledge disciplines, and technologies to assemble necro-biographies and eradicate the biographical subjects, based on biographies that are not in the public domain and thus function without accountability, except after the crucial fact, when various media report civilian/non-combatant deaths which result from either bad "intel" (i.e., faulty biographical work) or, as is also frequently the case, indifference about "collateral deaths" (innocent people near the targets). Moreover, few who are privy to the actual sighting of deaths receive media time to register their sentiments. The worldwide sighting of a death-by-assassination is a rare event. Reporting on one, the writer/photographer Teju Cole brings us back to the moment, captured in worldwide media, of Eddie Adams's iconic photograph of General Nguyen Ngoc Loan's fatal shot to the head of a Viet Cong commander, Nguyen Van Lem. Many saw it at the time and have seen it since. However, as Cole remarks, "The picture was remarkable for the rarity of its achievement, in recording the last moment, unscripted and hardly antici- pated, of someone's life. But when you see death mediated in this way, pinned down with such dramatic flair, the star is likely to be death itself and not the human who dies."[64] As I turn to a focus on the documenting of deaths of innocents, my example, Robert Greenwald's *Unmanned: America's Drone Wars*, makes the victims – rather than death – the stars.

Robert Greenwald's Counter-Biographies

As I have noted, in response to the CIA's biographical fic- tions, my question is about the kind of media within which one can mount a critique of the "war on terror's" necro- biographies. While the Showtime television series *Home- land* is one, there is a much more compelling alternative, which provides the names of actual victims rather than mere victim prototypes. Robert Greenwald's *Unmanned: America's Drone Wars* provides a series of counter- biographies that effectively return the CIA's anthropologi- cal gaze. It begins with a brief autobiography by Brandon Bryant, shown in close-up on-screen as he recounts details of an unremarkable childhood, his decision to enter the air force (he wanted a reprieve from mounting student loans), and his position as a drone warfare sensor, directing missiles against those designated as terrorists (the job involves "killing people," he's told). Remorseful by the time he has left the air force, he testifies to the arbitrariness of the targeting in which he was involved. Revisited in the documentary after Pakistani victims are shown and their relatives and friends testify on screen to the misapprehensions that led to their targeting, Bryant recounts an episode of firing on and killing three men whose eligibility for eradication consisted only in the fact that they were walking around, carrying rifles. He notes that, as a resident of Montana, it was not unusual to see men walking around with rifles and wonders why the same scenario in Pakistan warrants killing them. In effect, as a drone sensor, Bryant was watching a documentary about deaths for which he was partly responsible in real time. The effect of recalling his witnessing of those on-screen deaths is registered on his face as the camera zooms closer (Figure 5.2), creating what Deleuze calls an "affection image...the way in which the subject perceives itself, or rather experiences itself or feels itself, from the 'inside.' "[65]

Figure 5.2 Brandon Bryant

The other most significant bio in Greenwald's documentary is of a 16-year-old high-school student, Tariq Aziz,
who is targeted and killed while in a car with his brother
and cousins on their way to a soccer team recruitment. It
becomes apparent that Tariq's CIA bio had thickened to
the point where he was eligible for eradication. What data
were available to constitute Tariq as a terrorist? As visuals
of his movements and local testimony indicate, he attended
a large public meeting in Islamabad in which tribal elders,
Pakistani officials, other civic leaders, political candidates,
and interested members of the public were present in order
to share information about the drone killing of innocent
civilians (for example, one of Tariq's cousins) and to
protest the drone program.

As testimony indicates, it is likely that an "informant"
turned over Tariq's name to the CIA (for pay, as is the case
with the CIA's informant practice). That information,
along with the CIA's anthropological conceits, made a
16-year-old high-school student, whose "crime" was the
political activism of attending a public meeting, a victim
of extra-judicial killing, i.e., a summary execution, without
a chance to testify about his intentions and behavior.
Unlike what was available to the CIA and the rest of the
targeting *dispositif* involved in the targeting decision,
viewers of the documentary get to know this innocent
high-school student – a soccer player with good defensive
talent, a youngster with a good sense of humor, a high-
school student admired by his teacher Mr Wali, and a
politically energized citizen, prompted to get involved after
a cousin dies in a drone attack.

Much of what the documentary conveys is done with
images. In one scene, the camera closes in on a soccer ball,
an important cultural object that functions in both Pakistani culture in general and specifically in Tariq's filmed
biography. The sequence pulls back to show a large enough
scene to include both the ball and a plane flying overhead
(Figure 5.3). On the one hand, there is extensive ethnographic information that one can discern with interviews

Figure 5.3 Soccer ball and overhead plane

of people who knew the victims of drone attacks and can testify to the cultural practices on the ground (where the soccer ball sits). On the other is the distant anthropology of the CIA-military gaze, represented by a plane flying thousands of feet over the scene. There is a similar juxtaposition – first, a landscape scene filmed from above through the surveillance lens of a drone, followed by a tracking shot on the ground as a local landscape is seen from a car window, representing Tariq's journey to the rally in Islamabad.

Ultimately, in Tariq's case, as in the case of the documentary's other notable coverage of the drone attack on a "Jirga" (the democratic assemblage noted above, in which tribal elders gather with townspeople to settle local disputes) in the North Pakistan town of Datta Khel, the intelligence was misguided. As testimony and images show, within 40 minutes of the start of the meeting, drone attacks kill most of the participants, and subsequent interviews with Pakistani officials (for example, the former ambassador to the United States) and the relatives of the victims indicate that a major cultural event was interpreted as a terrorist plot. Interspersed with the testimonies about the

nature of the cultural event and the loss experienced by
the relatives (mostly sons of tribal elders whose bodies
were in fragments to the point where one son could not
distinguish his father's feet from his hands), are on-screen
remarks by US officials who dispense the administration's
"truth weapons" to legitimate the murders – e.g., "There's
every indication that this was a group of terrorists, not a
charity car wash in the Pakistani hinterlands." (Tellingly,
the anonymous official spokespersons are screening Pakistani culture through their own cultural practices.)
However irrational past wars may have been, the intelligibility demands involved in friend–enemy identification
were relatively clear because the conflicts involved states
versus states. In the case of the "war on terror," ambigui-
ties abound and arbitrary assassination decisions, based
on sketchy information that construes individuals as
enemies, are the rule.

Subjecting America's drone warfare to "a philosophical
investigation," Chamayou refers to "a crisis of intelligibility" because drone warfare defies the "established categories" that have hitherto been applied to warfare.[66]
Chamayou's emphasis is on the way the new militarized
gaze has constituted parts of the world as a hostile environment viewed through the lens of CIA anthropology and
the resultant apparatuses constructed to implement their
perspective. Robert Greenwald's documentary constitutes
a return of that gaze. As the documentary shows, the
implementation of that gaze has created precarious lives
and the deaths of many innocents, while what the US
public hears are official lies – for example, CIA head
William Brennan at a press conference: "In the last year
there hasn't been a single collateral death." Here is the
documentary's main juxtaposition. On the day that Tariq
Aziz was murdered, an innocent 16-year-old high-school
student was also murdered (as his high-school teacher,
Wali, points out on screen). Cut to the *Washington Post*'s
reporter Karen de Young: "I asked the CIA about the strike
and they said no child was killed." The truth weapon

remains a major part of the United States' arsenal. While Greenwald's documentary provides specific names, there is other documentation that has given the lie to the United States' truth weapon. An online site, produced by a team at "Pitch Interactive," a California-based studio that creates visualization technology, provides a visualization of every drone attack in Pakistan between 2004 and 2013. The data show that "fewer than 2 percent of [the more than 3,000] drone deaths have been 'high profile targets,' and 'the rest are civilians, children and alleged combatants' "[67] – where that last category "is really a very grey area," according to Wesley Grubbs, the leader of the Pitch Interactive team. "The Obama administration would call these people 'military combatants' because they are of-age males."[68]

"All Plots End in Death"

The quoted heading belongs to the novelist Don DeLillo, who uses it more than once (for example, in both his *White Noise* (1985) and *Libra* (1988), doubtless because he likes its ambiguity (all lives end in death and so do the fictional ones he plots). To situate *my* plot, the contingencies that mark innocent victims for death, as the United States' employed killers (drone sensors and pilots) are brought into relationships with their victims (not only those selected for targeted assassination but also those in the vicinity who die as well), I want to rehearse a fictional scenario of an earlier type of encounter that ends in death. In the face of the present "time-space compression," in which distant lives are suddenly connected, Russell Banks's novel *Continental Drift*, a story that takes place at the beginning of the 1980s, brings us back to an earlier temporality. Two characters whose lives are mapped throughout the novel drift toward their destinations. The encounter between them, as global forces affect their fates, takes place near the end of the narrative, when the plot ends in death.

Banks likens the trajectories of their movements to geo-physical, planetary movement: "It's as if the creatures residing on this planet, in these years, the human creatures, millions of them traveling singly and in families, in clans and tribes, traveling sometimes as entire nations, were a subsystem inside the larger system of currents and tides, of winds and weather, of drifting continents and sifting, uplifting, grinding, cracking land masses."[69]

Like Greenwald's documentary, Banks's novel is presented as a dual biography. The novel's narrative has two moving bodies, those of an everyman, Bob Dubois, an oil-burner repairman from New Hampshire, moving for economic reasons, and Vanise Dorsinville, a Haitian refugee, moving for political reasons. Near the end of the tale, they meet off the coast of Florida (on Bob's boat that is running Haitian refugees to Florida) after both struggle through dangerous and emotionally fraught experiences of adaptation to their changing environments – Bob leaving New Hampshire for Florida to work in his brother's liquor store, then drifting into the fishing business and thence to running illegal migrants when the fishing becomes unprofitable, and Vanise making her way from Haiti with her child and nephew, hopscotching through the Caribbean, while abused and exploited before landing in Florida. The concept of "drift" marks the relatively slow pace through which the encounter eventuates. Bob and Vanise, two diasporic bodies (both with French surnames, which reflect earlier migrations) articulate Banks's view of a planet with which he privileges flows of people rather than geopolitical units and emphasizes the contingencies of encounter, as economic and political forces impel bodies to move from one place to another. Apart from what their stories suggest about the evolution of the US ethnoscape – a "people" is a product not of the evolution of a natural community but rather of overlapping diasporas and identity-shaping encounters – is what it says about the temporality of some encounters in the early 1980s, when there was a flow of Haitian refugees to the United States and at the same time a moment of US domestic bodies, moving as they sought economic survival. The "drift" of the two bodies, and its consummation in their encounter (and ultimately in Bob's death when he tries to find Vanise to give her his ill-gotten gains) yields a telling contrast. The pace of the movement that brought Bob and Vanise's bodies into contact contrasts dramatically with the temporality involved in today's "time-space compression" which unites the drone sensor and pilot with their targets.

Nevertheless, Bob Dubois' ethical moment at the end of Banks's novel – his sense of guilt for exploiting Haitian refugees, one of whom dies (Vanise's nephew) after Bob's crewman throws the refugees off the boat when a coast-guard patrol shows up – is similar to what is experienced by Brandon Bryant, whose bio occupies part of Greenwald's documentary. Bryant, like Banks's Dubois, found himself in his occupation as a result of economic privation, in his case a daunting accumulation of college loans. Although loans put temporality into economy, allowing one to defer debt, there remains a complex calculation about the viability of accumulating debt. One has to gauge a relationship between one's biological clock and the repayment period. Thus, although Bryant reports on liking to read comics that pitted good guys against bad guys, that binary was not what drove him to be a killer. Ambivalent from the beginning about his assignment, the work turned out to be stressful. Richard Maxwell effectively captures Bryant's experience: "Surveillance is tough work ... working conditions can include any combination of the following: stress ... irregular hours, and a heavy toll on private life." Moreover, "On top of the physical and psychological strain, a surveillance worker must also possess great self-discipline to control unproductive ethical impulses to look away, to perceive innocence instead of guilt, to see a friend not a foe, to accept the ineffable and resist the probable."[70] Referring to how the task was characterized for him, "You kill people," Bryant says, "I worried about it; can I do this, can I pull the trigger? (I'm actually not pulling the trigger;

I'm guiding the missile in, but it's more or less the same thing)." Ultimately, Bryant was unable to "control unproductive ethical impulses." A grim-faced Bryant, brought back later in the documentary, reports the incident in which he guided a missile that hit the three men (noted on p. 147) carrying what appeared to be weapons, in the mountains of Pakistan. Two are killed instantly while a third is mortally wounded. Bryant recounts his death in graphic detail. He saw a pool of blood cooling on the ground as the victim rolled around in agony:

> We watched the guy turn the same color as the ground as he bled out. I could almost see his facial expression. I could almost see his mouth open, crying out. Maybe he cursed us, or maybe he asked Allah for forgiveness for us. Who knows what he said or thought. It wasn't pretty whatever it was. It was shock and trauma, and his ears were probably ringing. He was bleeding out and he was in agony. I didn't know how to react. No one teaches you how to react; they teach you how to do it. They ignore the reaction part. I wished I never contributed to that.

Ethical Space and the Sight of and Framing of Death

I want to note one moment when the Obama administration's "truth weapon" was suspended. the *New York Times* reported that, "The families of an anti-Qaeda cleric and a police officer killed in an American drone strike in Yemen filed suit in federal court in Washington on Sunday night, asking the court to declare that the strike was unlawful."[71] Although, not surprisingly, the claim has gone unanswered, one of the plaintiff's observations is telling. It cites President Obama's decision in April to publicly disclose that a separate American strike, on a Qaeda compound in Pakistan, had inadvertently killed two western hostages, an American and an Italian. The lawsuit notes that President Obama said at the time that the hostages' "families deserve to know the truth" and that the United States was willing "to confront squarely our imperfections and to learn from our mistakes" and goes on to state, "There is a simple question at the heart of this claim...The president has now admitted to killing innocent Americans and Italians with drones; why are the bereaved families of innocent Yemenis less entitled to the truth?"

The administration's momentary suspension of its war on truth operates within what I have elsewhere termed a "moral cartography" within which the spatial identities of some groups (for example, those outside of "the West") are deemed less worthy of moral solicitude.[72] The administration's "morality-delegating spatial unconscious"[73] constitutes an update to what Joseph Conrad deemed *his* contemporary stage in geography. Reacting to the excesses of colonial violence by western nations, he deemed his epoch an age of "geography triumphant," a period of the spread of European settlement.[74] The current stage in geographic violence takes a different form, perhaps best termed "geography securitized." Rather than a spread of settlement, we live in what Rey Chow refers to as "the age of the world target," in which there is a spread of targeting rather than settlement.[75] Inasmuch as that geography is overlaid with the United States' contemporary map of moral solicitude (within which some identities are worthy of moral solicitude and others can be sacrificed), we have the warrants in place for Obama's suspension of the truth weapon.

Tariq Aziz (Figure 5.4) didn't get to provide his assessment of the arbitrariness of his drone killing. That task is taken up in Greenwald's documentary. The flagrant violations of his rights (to testify against the charges that led to his death warrant) and his body (destroyed on the basis of biographical whims) receive testimony from those who knew him: family members, a teacher, peace activists, and reporters. What we see of Tariq are photos of a smiling young man. The photos' appearances, as moments in the

Figure 5.4 Tariq Aziz

documentary, constitute them as double events. In the context of their origin, they represent events of family and/ or clan cohesion, moments of affective belonging. Their inclusion in Greenwald's composition of shots, images, and commentaries constitutes them as second events, in this case as counter-visions to what is seen through drone surveillance as an articulation of another "composition" (for the CIA what is seen is a function of how they compose the Pakistani life-world).[76] What do *we* see as viewers of the documentary? To borrow from Roland Barthes (on the temporality of the photo portrait of someone who has died), we "observe with horror an anterior future of which death is the stake."[77] Other victims, mostly nameless, whom the CIA's "compositions" have also transformed from earthly live presences into will-have-beens appear anonymously as corpses. Their innocence is verified through the work of the journalist/photographer Noor Behram, who collected evidence in Waziristan of the civilian deaths, which he says, "the CIA and US government can't disprove" (his photos of the dead – many women and children – appear on-screen as he testifies).

Whereas Brandon Bryant offers an ethical position through his direct testimony, Robert Greenwald's documentary as a whole articulates an ethics through the montage of shots, images, and testimonies – for example in the scene in which he juxtaposes an overhead, satellite-eye view of the landscape-as-space-for-targeting, and the tracking shot of Tariq's journey from his village to a peaceful assembly in Islamabad. Jean-Luc Godard's suggestion, noted in chapter 2, about the film *Hiroshima Mon Amour* applies well here. When asked whether the film is jarring aesthetically or morally, Godard insisted that the aesthetic and moral aspects of the film coincide: "Tracking shots *are* a question of morality."[78]

There is therefore a dual ethical engine in the aesthetics of the documentary as it testifies to death's "ferocious reality."[79] One part is generated by Brandon Bryant, emerging through the way he was powerfully affected by the sight of the death of the man who "bled out" in a matter of minutes as a result of the missile he sent. As Vivian Sobchack suggests, inasmuch as what we attach to a natural death is an extended *durée*, "the abrupt transformation of the animated body into an inanimate corpse denies formal reason and connotes the 'irrationality,' 'arbitrariness,' and 'unfairness' of death."[80] To repeat: as Bryant notes as he contemplates the criteria that marked the three men for death from the point of view of one who has lived in Montana, it was a common sight, attracting no moral obloquy, to see men walking around with guns. Yet here he was asked to regard men in the mountains with guns as enemies. As he narrates his rejection of his deadly role and his remorse for the deaths in which he participated, his face carries as much of the burden of his ethical challenge as his words. Greenwald's camera zooms in for a close-up during the narration, inviting the viewer to adopt the horror written on his face, which at very close range loses its individuation. As Deleuze suggests, "the close-up of the face acts not through the individuality of a role or of a character, or even through the personality of the

actor...[rather] the close-up makes the face the pure building material...[part of a] "relationship...to other shots
and to other types of images."[81]

Bryant's ethical contribution is therefore incorporated
as part of Greenwald's. His recounting of his ethical
moment devolves into the ethical framing of the documentary as a whole. Through its composition or form, the
documentary is effectively "inscribing ethical space," a
space of rapid annihilation with a series of abrupt killings
that transform the living – daughters, sons, fathers,
mothers, and cousins – into the dead. Through the ways
in which it witnesses death's "ferocious reality" and the
cynical justifications used to exonerate the perpetrators
(US officials and their apparatuses of "knowledge production" and violent implementation), Greenwald's *Unmanned:
America's Drone War* documents and mounts an ethico-
political challenge to a catastrophic, unjust war on (mostly)
civilian non-combatants, which US officials legitimate with
their truth weapons (legitimations that the mainstream
media reproduce as they recycle the discourse of terrorism). The documentary returns the militarized gaze, articulated through drone perception, with a *"humane gaze,"*[82]
restoring an interpersonal intimacy surrounding the lives
of victims that drone-oriented perception cannot heed.

To situate the pseudo-biographical intelligence that
frames the drone-oriented perception, I want to summon
more words from the writer Don DeLillo, who decades
ago (as he prepared to write his novelistic biography of
Lee Harvey Oswald) wrote a brief essay, entitled "American Blood," about American assassins of public figures.
Apropos of CIA "knowledge production," DeLillo's essay
contains a prescient imaginative gloss on the way Oswald
was scripted by "the agency":

> "Lee Harvey Oswald" often seems a secret design worked
> out by men who will never surface...a procedural diagram,
> a course in fabricated biography. Who put him together?
> He is not an actor so much as he is a character, a fictional

character who first emerges in the year 1957...Oswald seems scripted out of doctored photos, tourist cards, change-of-address cards, mail-order forms, visa applications, altered signatures, pseudonyms.[83]

Conclusion: Media Encounters

Don DeLillo's imaginative construction of a CIA-invented biography of Lee Harvey Oswald is but one instance of the way the arts, especially literature and film (both fictional and documentary), "bear" what Marco Abel calls, "the *pedagogical* potential for activating an *ethical* mode of encounter with violence."[84] In light of the potential effects of Robert Greenwald's documentary film *Unmanned*, which challenges the violence of the drone *dispositif*'s role in the contemporary "war on terror," I want to add that film in particular mounts a powerful critique because of its ability to generate counter-images within narratives that challenge official truth weapons. To evoke once more the "weapons sublime." As I have suggested, what Greenwald's documentary especially challenges is the drone's-eye view's relay of the security gaze. To give that challenge more specificity, I refer to Nasser Hussain's analysis of the phenomenology of a drone strike. He points out, citing one of the drone program's military apologists (a retired colonel), that a drone hovers for a while over its selected target, adding "oversight" with the prolonged hovering that produces a buzzing that terrorizes much of the population of Pakistan. (As *Unmanned* attests, there is a degree of oversight added to mere sight.) However, because drones operate only in a "visual economy" where sound is not available to accompany vision, "the layers of supervision effectively evacuate the world of sound and the interpersonal reality that sound produces."[85]

Moreover, the public perception of drone strikes arises from the phenomenology of the public point of view: "We have become too accustomed to seeing from the air, which violates all the familiar geometry and perspective of our mundane, grounded vision."[86] That phenomenology is in part constitutive of what I referred to at the outset of this chapter as "the weapons sublime": the problem of connecting one's local world of weapons production and deployment to the distant life-world of blurred boundaries between enemies and non-combatants. In effect, what Greenwald's documentary supplies is a counter-weapon. Borrowing from and re-inflecting Walter Benjamin's enduringly relevant analysis of the power of a work of art (in his "The Work of Art in the Age of Mechanical Reproduction"), I offer here a re-inflection: "the work of art in the age of drone's-eye vision," invoking especially Benjamin's notion of the "shock effect" of film-as-counter-weapon. Reflecting on the effect of the Dadaists, Benjamin wrote:

> From an alluring appearance or persuasive structure of sound the work of art of the Dadaists became an instrument of ballistics. It hit the spectator like a bullet... Let us compare the screen on which a film unfolds with the canvas of a painting. The painting invites the spectator to contemplation; before it the spectator can abandon himself to his associations. Before the movie frame he cannot do so. No sooner has his eye grasped a scene than it is already changed. It cannot be arrested. This constitutes the shock effect of the film, which, like all shocks, should be cushioned by heightened presence of mind. By means of its technical structure, the film has taken the physical shock effect out of the wrappers in which Dadaism had, as it were, kept it inside the moral shock effect.[87]

Ultimately, *Unmanned* offers an encounter of technics – that associated with the weapons of war, challenged by the technics of cinema. The perceptual violence (followed by implemented violence) of drone technology becomes shockingly evident when encountered by the way the technology of cinema restores what drone perception evacuates.

Afterword

Pursued by the Sublime

As my analyses of politics and the temporalization of events proceeded through the various chapters, the concept of the sublime kept showing up unbidden. I ended chapter 4 with a focus on the "sweatshop sublime," and our inattention to the production end of the commodity chain (the problem of sustaining an imagination that connects our local, small world to the commodity chain that stretches out in a larger world of interdependence that makes available what we consume) and began chapter 5 noting the difficulty of comprehending another vast system, the "weapons sublime" (a reversal of the direction of the commodity chain where something produced locally, in our small world, impacts a larger world of vulnerable "consumers" – people abroad who are targeted by weapons launched from our domestic space). The sublime also pursued me in earlier chapters – in chapter 2, where I found myself referring to the "nuclear sublime" and noting that the atomic bomb dropped on Hiroshima was an overwhelming violence compressed into a single instant. The temporality of that event was unique and sublime because it was not, as Kyo Maclear (whom I quoted) wrote, "experienced as the cumulative result of protracted battles. There was no gradual interval in which to wrestle with the disruptive rhythm of 'conventional' war on everyday life." Rather, "the physical force of [the] disaster overwhelmed comprehension by virtue of [its] sheer and sudden magnitude."[1] And in chapter 3, in my analysis of the aftermath of Hurricane Katrina, I referred to the "racial sublime," a vast, almost incomprehensible system of racial discrimination and violence (incomprehensible for much of the white population, that is) which was starkly revealed in media images after the hurricane. The nature of that sublime is well captured, as I noted, in the words of Clyde Woods who marked the stunning revelation for those who had been hitherto obtuse about the magnitude of the immiseration of much of black America: "The disasters surrounding Hurricane Katrina revealed an impaired contemporary social vision of every segment of society. Despite mountains of communication and surveillance devices, America was still shocked by the revelation of impoverishment, racism, brutality, corruption, and official neglect in a place it thought it knew intimately."[2]

An About-Face

Since the pursuit has been duly noted, in this brief afterword I turn around and face the sublime in order to highlight an important part of my analysis, the role of documentary genres in resurrecting and re-inflecting events. For that purpose, I heed a crucial part of Immanuel Kant's approach to aesthetic comprehension in his "Analytic of the Sublime," where he elucidates the temporality involved in the experience of the sublime, as the subject undergoes the process of moving from the initial apprehension of a sublime event to a degree of comprehension (where what initially strikes and confounds the subject's imagination yields – in Kant's narrative – to the higher faculty of reason). In his discussion of the interplay between apprehension and comprehension that an encounter with the sublime precipitates, Kant refers to a breakdown that imperils comprehension. Treating the temporality of the sublime experience, Kant notes that the first moments in one's apprehension of a "sublime" (*"absolutely great"*[3] object or event) attenuate because "apprehension has reached a point beyond which the representation of sensuous intuition in the case of the parts first apprehended begin to disappear from the imagination as this advances to the apprehension of yet others,... and for comprehension we get a maximum which the imagination cannot exceed."[4]

Kant's consciousness-centered approach to experience – as a dynamic of apprehension/comprehension – is first presented in his *Critique of Pure Reason* where he renders the imagination involved in understanding (an "inner sense") as a progressive sequence of synthesis ultimately governed by a concept emerging from the understanding. As Rudolf Makkreel summarizes the earlier critique, "The imagination is bound by a progressive form of time – a linear sequence which moves on incessantly,"[5] resulting in a concept provided by the understanding. In contrast, in the case of the aesthetic comprehension that Kant analyzes in *The Critique of Judgment*, there is no concept to consummate comprehension. Instead, there is an interplay of imagination and reason, once imagination reaches its limit. At that point, comprehension is a mere "instant of what was successively apprehended" and is seen by Kant as "a retrogression that removes the time-condition in the progression of the imagination, and renders *co-existence* intuitable [as a]... time series [with which it]... does violence to the internal sense."[6] As Makkreel points out, in treating "the imaginative regress which annihilates the condition of time," Kant refers to "comprehension in an instant [*Augenblick*: at one glance]," which "has a technical meaning which is better brought out by translating it as 'instant.'"[7]

Certainly, Kyo Maclear's rendering of the initial comprehension of the nuclear explosion in Hiroshima accords

with Kant's "instant." (To repeat her statement) "There
was no gradual interval in which to wrestle with the disruptive rhythm of 'conventional' war on everyday life."
Rather, "the physical force of [the] disaster overwhelmed
comprehension by virtue of [its] sheer and sudden magnitude." However, as is pointed out in chapter 2, subsequent
contemplation of the Hiroshima experience in various
documentary genres have turned the sublime moment into
a continuing will-have-been. Moreover, while for Kant the
experience of the sublime is ultimately comprehended
without resort to a unifying concept, the subsequent reproduction and re-inflection of Hiroshima has generated successively new concepts. As Deleuze points out, as history
unfolds, each new concept "displaces the field of intelligibility, modifying conditions of the problem we pose for
ourselves."[8]

As my focus on the "modifying conditions" that new
concepts and "altered fields of intelligibility" has proceeded with turns to a variety of documentary genres, the
temporality involved in the experience of events has
belonged to documentary time rather than the subjective
instant involved in the interval between apprehension
and comprehension. "Documentary time," a "constructed
temporality"[9] as Malin Wahlberg suggests, displaces mentality with "a technology of memory"[10] – as, for example,
in the case of cinematic documentaries within which events
are reframed but not closed, for the documentary maker
cannot be assured of achieving what Immanuel Kant
desired to achieve in his approach to aesthetic comprehension, an enduring common sense (*sensus communis*)
or "subjective finality." Inasmuch as "events" are never
closed, I'll let Chris Marker (whose semi documentary,
Level Five, inaugurates my investigation) have the last
word: "you never know what you are actually filming."[11]

Notes

Preface

1 C. Wright Mills, "Review of Franz Neumann's *Behemoth: The Structure and Function of National Socialism 1933–1944*," *Partisan Review*. Online at: http://www.wbenjamin.org/Behemoth.html.

2 The quotation is from Paul Patton, "The World Seen from Within: Deleuze and the Philosophy of Events," *Theory & Event* 1(1) (1997). Online at: http://muse.jhu.edu/journals/theory_and_event/summary/v001/1.1patton.html.

3 For more specification of the perspective, see Gilles Deleuze and Felix Guattari, *What is Philosophy?*, trans. Hugh Tomlinson and Graham Burchell (New York: Columbia University Press, 1994).

4 Michel Foucault, *The Archaeology of Knowledge*, trans. A. M. Sheridan Smith (New York: Pantheon, 1972), 120.

5 Michel Foucault, *Manet and the Object of Painting*, trans. M. Barr (London: Tate, 2009), 32.

6 Ibid., 16.

7 Primo Levi, *The Reawakening*, trans. Stuart Woolf (New York: Collier, 1987), 11.

8 Ibid. Unbeknownst to Levi (who was not privy to Czech culture), Hurbinek is likely based on the character "Hurvinek," a popular figure from the Czech puppet theater. The child's sounds that Levi reports are likely based on Czech as well (e.g., *maso* is the Czech word for meat and *maslo* is the word for butter). I owe those insights to Professor Petr Kouba of the Philosophy and Religious Studies Institute of Charles University in Prague.

9 Imre Kertész, *The Holocaust as Culture*, trans. Thomas Cooper (Chicago: Seagull Books, 2011), 43.

10 Slavoj Žižek, *Event: A Philosophical Journey through a Concept* (Brooklyn, NY: Melville House, 2014), ebook, loc. 114.

11 See Rosalyn Deutsche, *Hiroshima after Iraq: Three Studies in Art and War* (New York: Columbia University Press, 2010).
12 See Claude Romano, *Event and Time*, trans. Stephen E. Lewis (New York: Fordham University Press, 2014), xi.
13 The quotation is from Kaja Silverman, "Waiting, Hoping, among the Ruins of All the Best," in Bill Nichols and Michael Renov (eds), *Cinema's Alchemist: The Films of Péter Forgács* (Minneapolis: University of Minnesota Press, 2011), ebook, loc. 1416.
14 Michael Eric Dyson, "Racial Terror, Fast and Slow," *The New York Times*. Online at: http://www.nytimes.com/2015/04/17/opinion/racial-terror-fast-and-slow.html?_r=0.
15 See Michael J. Shapiro, "National Times and Other Times: Re-Thinking Citizenship," *Cultural Studies* 14(1) (January) (2000), 79–98.
16 Thomas Pynchon, *Mason & Dixon* (New York: Henry Holt, 1997), 195.
17 Michel Foucault, "Introduction" to Georges Canguilhem, *The Normal and the Pathological*, trans. Carolyn R. Fawcett (New York: Zone Books, 1989), 15.
18 Gilles Deleuze, *Cinema 2*, trans. Hugh Tomlinson and Robert Galeta (Minneapolis: University of Minnesota Press, 1989), 133.
19 For an analysis of the relationship between cinema genres and counter-history, see Marcia Landy, *Cinema & Counter-History* (Bloomington: Indiana University Press, 2015).

Chapter 1   Critical Temporalities: Thinking the Event

1 Milan Kundera, *Slowness* (London: Faber and Faber, 1996), 79.
2 Michael J. Shapiro, "Slow Looking: The Ethics and Politics of Aesthetics," a review essay in *Millennium* 37(1) (2008), 182.
3 The quotation is from Jacques Rancière's commentary on Jaar's installation, *Theater of Images*, in *Alfredo Jaar: La Politique Des Images* (Lausanne: jrp/ringier, 2008), 71.
4 Ibid., 76.
5 The expression "semi-documentary" belongs to Christa Blumlinger (quoting Marker). See "The Imaginary Documentary Image: Chris Marker's *Level Five*," *Image & Narrative* 11(1) (2010), 3.
6 The expression belongs to Howard Hampton in his review of *Level Five*, in *Film Comment*. Online at: http://www.filmcomment.com/article/review-level-five-chris-marker.
7 See Michael J. Shapiro, "Towards a Politics of Now-Time: Reading *Hoop Dreams* with Kubrick's *Barry Lyndon*," in *Cinematic Political Thought* (New York: New York University Press, 1999), 10–38.
8 I borrow the term "legibility" from Walter Benjamin, who used it in his approach to the philosophy of historical time. See his "Theses on the Philosophy of History," in Hannah Arendt (ed.), *Illuminations*, trans. Harry Zone (New York: Schocken, 1968), 254–5.

9 Jean-François Lyotard, *Des Dispositif Pulsionnels* (Paris: Christian Bourgeois, 1980), 170–1, my translation.

10 The expression belongs to Ralph Waldo Emerson. See his "Nature," in *Emerson's Essays* (New York: Harper & Row, 1951), 397.

11 For a good critical narrative of the relevant intellectual history, see Peter Osborne, *The Politics of Time: Modernity and the Avant-Garde* (London: Verso, 2011).

12 Benjamin, "Theses on the Philosophy of History," 255.

13 See for example Michel Foucault, "Language to Infinity," in Donald Bouchard (ed.), *Language, Counter-Memory, Practice* (Ithaca, NY: Cornell University Press, 1977), 53–67.

14 The quotations are from Werner Hamacher, "'Now': Walter Benjamin on Historical Time," in Heidrun Friese (ed.), *The Moment: Time and Rupture in Modern Thought* (Liverpool: Liverpool University Press, 2001), 170.

15 W. E. B. Du Bois, *Black Reconstruction: An Essay Toward a History of the Part Which Black Folk Played in the Attempt to Reconstruct Democracy in America: 1860–1880* (New York: Harcourt, Brace and Company, 1935), 725.

16 Ibid., 350.

17 Ibid., 353.

18 Ibid., 352.

19 Hamacher, "'Now': Walter Benjamin on Historical Time," 171.

20 As he puts it in his earlier work on archaeology, "Instead of exploring the consciousness/knowledge (*connaissance*)/science axis (which cannot escape subjectivity), archaeology explores the discursive practice/knowledge (*savoir*)/science axis": Foucault, *The Archaeology of Knowledge*, 183.

21 Shapiro, "Towards a Politics of Now-Time," 16.

22 Michel Foucault, "What is Critique?" in Sylvere Lotringer (ed.), *The Politics of Truth* (New York: Semiotext(e), 2007), 59.

23 Ibid., 66.

24 Michel Foucault, "About the Concept of the 'Dangerous Individual' in 19th-Century Legal Psychiatry," *Journal of Law and Psychiatry* 1 (1978), 2.

25 Ibid., 6.

26 Michel Foucault, "Governmentality," in Graham Burchell et al. (eds), *The Foucault Effect* (Chicago: University of Chicago Press, 1991), 100.

27 See Norbert Elias, "Sport as a Sociological Problem," in Norbert Elias and Eric Dunning (eds), *Quest For Excitement* (Oxford: Basil Blackwell, 1986), 126–49.

28 See Johan Huizinga, *Homo Ludens* (Boston: Beacon Press, 1955).

29 Those moments are reported in Dennis Brailsford, *Sport, Time and Society* (New York: Routledge, 1991).

30 The quotation is from Janet Lever and Stanton Wheeler, "Mass Media and the Experience of Sport," *Communication Research* 20 (1993), 125.

31 The quotations are from Stuart Elden's translation in "Reading Genealogy as Historical Ontology," in Alan Michman and Alan Rosenberg (eds), *Foucault and Heidegger: Critical Encounters* (Minneapolis: University of Minnesota Press, 2003), 200.
32 See Gilles Deleuze, *The Logic of Sense*, trans. Mark Lester and Charles Stivale (New York: Columbia University Press, 1990).
33 Ibid., 147.
34 The quotation is from Deleuze's analysis of Leibniz: Gilles Deleuze, *The Fold, Leibniz and the Baroque*, trans. Tom Conley (Minneapolis: University of Minnesota Press, 1992), 86.
35 For a good summary treatment, see Levi R. Bryant, "The Ethics of the Event: Deleuze and Ethics without Αρχή," in Nathan Jun and Daniel W. Smith (eds), *Deleuze and Ethics* (Edinburgh: Edinburgh University Press, 2011), 21–43.
36 This apt expression belongs to François Zourabichvili, *Deleuze: A Philosophy of the Event*, trans. Kieran Aarons (Edinburgh: Edinburgh University Press, 2012), 97.
37 Deleuze, *The Logic of Sense*, 161.
38 See Michael J. Shapiro, "The 'Musico-Literary' Aesthetics of Attachment and Resistance," in *Methods and Nations: Cultural Governance and the Indigenous Subject* (London: Routledge, 2004), 91.
39 The quotation is from Adam Gussow, *It Seems like Murder Here* (Chicago: The University of Chicago Press, 2002), 161. I quote it in my analysis of blues: "The Blues Subject," in Michael J. Shapiro, *Studies in Trans-Disciplinary Method: After the Aesthetic Turn* (New York: Routledge, 2012), 54.
40 The quotation is from David Schiff, *The Ellington Century* (Berkeley: University of California Press, 2012), 13.
41 Paul Gilroy, *Darker than Blue: On the Moral Economies of Black Atlantic Culture* (Harvard University Press, 2010), 131.
42 Ibid., 132.
43 See Coltrane's remarks on his *Alabama* reported in Sacha Feinstein, "From *Alabama* to *A Love Supreme*: The Evolution of a John Coltrane Poem," *The Southern Review* 23(2) (April, 1996), 315–27.
44 Jacques Attali, *Noise: The Political Economy of Music*, trans. Brian Massumi (Minneapolis: University of Minnesota Press, 1985), 58.
45 Shapiro, "The 'Musico-Literary' Aesthetics of Attachment and Resistance," 92.
46 Roman Jacobson and Morris Halle, *Fundamentals of Language* (The Hague: Mouton, 1971), 69.
47 Ibid., 74.
48 Henry Louis Gates, Jr, *The Signifying Monkey: A Theory of Afro-American Literary Criticism* (New York: Oxford University Press, 1988), 52.
49 The quotation is from Nathaniel Mackey, "Other: From Noun to Verb," in Krin Gabbard (ed.), *Jazz among the Discourses* (Durham, NC: Duke University Press, 1995), 83.

50 Ibid., 126.
51 The quotation is from Michael J. Shapiro, *Methods and Nations: Cultural Governance and the Indigenous Subject* (New York: Routledge, 2004), 94.
52 Duke Ellington, "Interview in Los Angeles: on *Jump for Joy*, Opera and Dissonance," in Mark Tucker (ed.), *The Duke Ellington Reader* (New York: Oxford University Press, 1993), 150.
53 Shapiro, *Methods and Nations*, 92.
54 Gilles Deleuze, *Difference and Repetition*, trans. Paul Patton (New York: Columbia University Press, 1994), 10.
55 Paul Ricoeur, *Time and Narrative* (Vol. 3), trans. Kathleen Blamey and David Pellauer (Chicago: University of Chicago Press, 1988), 128.
56 Ibid., 131.
57 Ibid., 132.
58 Jacques Rancière, "The Aesthetic Revolution and its Outcomes," *New Left Review* 14 (March–April, 2002), 143.
59 Ricoeur, *Time and Narrative* (Vol. 3), 112.
60 The quotation is from Stephen Kern, *The Culture of Time and Space: 1880–1918* (Cambridge, MA: Harvard University Press, 1983), 14.
61 Carlos Fuentes, "Writing in Time," *Democracy* 2 (1962), 61. I am repeating a quotation from an earlier discussion: Michael J. Shapiro, *The Time of the City: Politics, Philosophy and Genre* (London: Routledge, 2010), 115.
62 Fuentes, "Writing in Time," 61.
63 Gilles Deleuze, *Proust and Signs*, trans. Richard Howard (Minneapolis: University of Minnesota Press, 2000), 16.
64 Ibid., 17.
65 Fuentes, "Writing in Time," 72. Fuentes's observation receives analytic framing by M. M. Bakhtin in his discussion of "chronotopes," which articulates "the intrinsic connectedness of temporal and spatial relationships that is artistically expressed in literature": M. M. Bakhtin, "Forms of Time and of the Chronotope in the Novel," in Michael Holquist (trans.), *The Dialogic Imagination* (Austin: University of Texas Press, 1981), 84.
66 Carlos Fuentes, *Destiny and Desire*, trans. Edith Grossman (New York: Random House, 2011), 382.
67 Ibid.
68 Sergei Eisenstein "Dickens, Griffith, and Film Today," in *Essays in Film Theory*, trans. Jay Leyda (New York: Meridian, 1957), 216–17.
69 Shapiro, *Studies in Trans-Disciplinary Method*, 25. The internal quotation is from Gilles Deleuze, *Cinema 2: The Time Image*, trans. High Tomlinson and Robert Galeta (Minneapolis: University of Minnesota Press, 1989), 116.
70 Michael J. Shapiro, *Cinematic Geopolitics* (London: Routledge, 2009), 13.
71 Christopher Allen, *Art in Australia: From Colonization to Postmodernism* (London: Thames and Hudson, 1997), 12.
72 Ibid., 68.

73 The quotations are from Michael Renov, "Introduction: The Truth about Non-Fiction," in Michael Renov (ed.), *Theorizing Documentary* (New York: Routledge, 1993), 3.

74 See Henri Bergson, *Matter and Memory*, trans. Nancy Margaret Paul and W. Scott Palmer (London, Allen and Unwin, 1911), 275.

75 The quotation is from Maurizio Lazzarato, *Signs and Machines*, trans. Joshua David Jordan (New York: Semiotext(e), 2014), 110–11.

76 Shapiro, *Cinematic Geopolitics*, 3 (the internal quotation belongs to Jean-Paul Sartre).

77 Gilles Deleuze, *Bergsonism*, trans. Hugh Tomlinson and Barbara Habberjam (New York: Zone Books, 1991), 55.

78 Louis Althusser, *Philosophy of the Encounter: Later Writings, 1978–87*, trans. G. M. Goshgarian (New York: Verso, 2006), 174.

79 Laszlo Krasznahorkai, *The Melancholy of Resistance*, trans. George Szirtes (New York: New Directions, 1998), ebook, loc. 789.

80 The quotation is from Janice Lee and Jared Woodland, "Apocalypse Withheld: On Slowness & the Long Take in Béla Tarr's *Satantango*," *Entropy*. Online at: http://entropymag.org/apocalypse-withheld-on-slowness-the-long-take-in-bela-tarrs-satantango/.

81 The book version is in Krasznahorkai, *The Melancholy of Resistance*, 18.

82 Daniel Bensaïd, *Marx for Our Times*, trans. Gregory Elliott (New York: Verso, 2002), 72.

83 Steven Marchant, "Nothing Counts: Shot and Event in *Werckmeister Harmonies*," *New Cinemas: Journal of Contemporary Film* 7(2) (2009), 137.

84 Harun Farocki, "Workers Leaving the Factory," trans. Laurent Faasch-Ibrahim, *Senses of Cinema*. Online at: http://sensesofcinema.com/2002/harun-farocki/farocki_workers/.

85 The quotations are from Michael Renov, *The Subject of Documentary* (Minneapolis: University of Minnesota Press, 2004), 129.

86 The expression belongs to James Clifford, *The Predicament of Culture* (Cambridge, MA: Harvard University Press), 147.

87 Ibid.

88 The quotation is from Catherine Lupton, *Chris Marker: Memories of the Future* (London: Reaktion Books, 2005), ebook, loc. 3122.

89 Ibid.

90 The quotation is from Mark B. N. Hansen's rendering of Jan Patočka's materialist version of phenomenology: *Feed Forward: On the Future of Twenty-First-Century Media* (Chicago: University of Chicago Press, 2015), 68.

91 Ibid.

92 The expression belongs to Jack Reynolds in his analysis of Deleuze's ethics of the event: "Wounds and Scars: Deleuze on the Time and Ethics of the Event," *Deleuze Studies* 1(2) (2007), 145.

Chapter 2   Hiroshima Temporalities

1 Kenzaburo Oe, *Hiroshima Notes*, trans. David L. Swain and Toshi Yonezawa (New York: Marion Boyars 1995), 35.
2 The quotations are from Kyo Maclear, *Beclouded Vision: Hiroshima-Nagasaki and the Art of Witness* (Albany: State University of New York Press, 1999), 4.
3 See *Unforgettable Fire: Pictures Drawn by Atomic Bomb Survivors* (New York: Pantheon, 1977), 5.
4 Commentary and drawing by Yasuko Yamagata (age 49 at the time of the commentary) in ibid., 52.
5 Oe, *Hiroshima Notes*, 67.
6 The quotation is from Rosalyn Deutsche, *Hiroshima after Iraq: Three Studies in Art and War* (New York: Columbia University Press, 2010), 16.
7 The quotation is from a reading of Benjamin's concept of plastic temporality: Peter Fenves, *The Messianic Reduction: Walter Benjamin and the Shape of Time* (Stanford, CA: Stanford University Press, 2011), 3.
8 Walter Benjamin, "Two Poems by Friedrich Hölderlin," trans. S. Corngold, in *Walter Benjamin: Selected Writings 1913–1926* (Cambridge, MA: Harvard University Press, 1996), 31.
9 Oe, *Hiroshima Notes*, 23.
10 The quotation is from Jonathan Boulter, *Melancholy and the Archive: Trauma, History and Memory in the Contemporary Novel* (New York: Bloomsbury, 2013), 11.
11 Deutsche, *Hiroshima after Iraq*, 10.
12 Jean Domarchi, "Hiroshima Notre Amour," *Cahiers du Cinema* 97 (1959), 63.
13 Quoted in Carol Mavor, *Black and Blue* (Durham, NC: Duke University Press, 2012), 115.
14 Ibid.
15 The quotation is from Brent Steele, "Hiroshima: The Strange Case of Maintaining (US) Collective Memory." Paper delivered at the 2011 annual meeting of the International Studies Association, 1.
16 Masuji Ibuse, *Black Rain*, trans. John Bester (New York: Kodansha, 2012 [originally published in 1969]), 77.
17 Ibid., 44.
18 Ibid., 282.
19 Ibid., 168.
20 Ibid., 171.
21 Ibid., 211.
22 The quotation belongs to John Bester in his "Translator's Preface" to Ibuse's *Black Rain*, 6.
23 Ibuse, *Black Rain*, 149.
24 Jean-Luc Godard, "Hiroshima Notre Amour," *Cahiers du Cinema* 97 (1959), 62.
25 Imre Kertész, *Fatelessness*, trans. Tim Wilkinson (New York: Vintage, 2004), 165.

26 Mavor, *Black and Blue*, 117.
27 Deutsche, *Hiroshima after Iraq*, 21.
28 Ibid., 16.
29 Chi-Hui Yang, "Q&A with Linda Hattendorf on 'The Cats of Mirikitani,'" *Cinema Asian America*. Online at: http://my.xfinity.com/blogs/tv/2013/08/01/cinema-asian-america-qa-with-linda-hattendorf-on-the-cats-of-mirikitani/.
30 The quotation is from Jacques Derrida, *Archive Fever: A Freudian Impression*, trans. Eric Prenowitz (Chicago: University of Chicago Press, 1995), 3.
31 Achille Mbembe, "The Power of the Archive and its Limit," in Carolyn Hamilton et al. (eds), *Refiguring the Archive* (Dordrecht, Netherlands: Kluwer Academic Publishers, 2002), 19.
32 Derrida, *Archive Fever*, 3.
33 Gilles Deleuze, *Cinema 2: The Time-Image*, trans. Hugh Tomlinson (Minneapolis: University of Minnesota Press, 1989), 116.
34 Michael J. Shapiro, *Studies in Trans-Disciplinary Method: After the Aesthetic Turn* (New York: Routledge, 2012), 25.
35 Jacques Rancière, *The Future of the Image*, trans. G. Elliot (New York: Verso, 2007), 55.
36 Ibid., 53.
37 Benjamin, "Theses on the Philosophy of History," in Hannah Arendt (ed.), *Illuminations*, trans. Harry Zone (New York: Schocken, 1968), 259.
38 Justin Erik Halldór Smith, "The Great Extinction," *The Chronicle Review*. Online at: http://www.jehsmith.com/1/essays-for-the-chronicle-review.html.
39 John Hersey, *Hiroshima* (New York: Alfred A. Knopf, 1946), 96.
40 See, for example, Benjamin Medea, *Drone Warfare: Killing by Remote Control* (London: Verso, 2013) and Christian Enemark, *Armed Drones and the Ethics of War: Military Virtue in a Post-Heroic Age* (London: Routledge, 2013).
41 See Grégoire Chamayou, "The Manhunt Doctrine," *Radical Philosophy* 169 (Sept./Oct., 2011). Online at: http://www.radicalphilosophy.com/commentary/the-manhunt-doctrine.
42 Ibid.
43 Ibid.
44 See Michael J. Shapiro, *War Crimes, Atrocity, and Justice* (Cambridge, UK: Polity, 2015), ch. 3.
45 See Spencer Ackerman, "CIA Drones Kill Large Groups without Knowing Who They Are," *Wired*. Online at: http://www.wired.com/dangerroom/2011/11/cia-drones-marked-for-death/.
46 Robert Albro and Hugh Gusterson, "Do No Harm," in *C4!SA Journal* 4/25/2012. Online at: http://www.defensenews.com/article/20120425/C4ISR02/304250001/Commentary-8216-Do-No-Harm-8217-html.
47 Michel Foucault, *Society Must Be Defended*, trans. David Macey (New York: Picador, 2003), 54–5.
48 See the Stanford-NYU investigation: "Living Under Drones: Death, Injury, and Trauma to Civilians from US Drone Practices in Pakistan,"

by the International Human Rights and Conflict Resolution Clinic of the Stanford Law School and the Global Justice Clinic of the NYU Law School.

49 Alice K. Ross, "Civilians Die in Reported Yemen Drone Strike as Weekend of Attacks Kill at Least 35," Projects. Online at: https://www.thebureauinvestigates.com/2014/04/21/civilians-die-in-yemen-drone-strike-as-weekend-of-attacks-kills-at-least-35/.

50 The quotations are from Sven Lindqvist, A History of Bombing, trans. Linda Haverty Rugg (New York: The New Press, 2001), 112.

51 Leuren Moret, "From Hiroshima to Iraq, 61 years of Uranium Wars." www.globalresearch.ca/from-hiroshima-to-iraq-61-years-uranium-wars/5949.

52 Sherwood Ross, "Radioactive Ammunition Fired in the Middle East May Claim More Lives than Hiroshima and Nagasaki," Democratic Underground.com. Online at: http://www.democraticunderground.com/discuss/duboard.php?az=view_all&address=389x2314187.

53 Those numbers are reported in Lindqvist, A History of Bombing, 112.

54 Rob Nixon, Slow Violence and the Environmentalism of the Poor (Cambridge, MA: Harvard University Press, 2011).

55 Milan Kundera, Slowness (London: Faber and Faber, 1996).

56 Victor Burgin, The Remembered Film (London: Reaktion Books, 2005).

57 Jill Bennett, Empathic Vision: Affect, Trauma, and Contemporary Art (Stanford, CA: Stanford University Press, 2005), 67.

58 Slavoj Žižek, "Kate's Choice, Or the Materialism of Henry James," in Slavoj Žižek (ed.), Lacan: The Silent Partners (New York: Verso, 2006), 290.

59 Jon Kertzer, "Time's Desire: Literature and the Temporality of Justice," Law, Culture and the Humanities 5(2) (2009), 269.

Chapter 3   Hurricane Katrina Bio-Temporalities

1 This version of my reaction is in Michael J. Shapiro, "The Discursive Spaces of Global Politics," Journal of Environmental Policy & Planning 7(3) (September, 2005), 227.

2 See Rob Nixon, Slow Violence and the Environmentalism of the Poor (Cambridge, MA: Harvard University Press, 2011).

3 See Scott Baldauf, "Bhopal Gas Tragedy Lives On, 20 Years Later," The Christian Science Monitor. Online at: http://www.csmonitor.com/2004/0504/p07s01-wosc.html.

4 Taipei Times (December 4, 2004), 5.

5 Newsweek. Online at: http://www.newsweek.com/india-after-30-years-bhopal-still-simmering-288144.

6 Steven Greenhouse, "U.S. Retailers Decline to Aid Factory Victims in Bangladesh," The New York Times (November 23, 2003), B1.

7 Shapiro, "The Discursive Spaces of Global Politics," 228.

8 Michel Houellebecq, The Map and the Territory, trans. Gavin Bowd (London: William Heinemann, 2011), 98.

9 See Judith Butler, *Frames of War: When is Life Grievable?* (New York: Verso, 2010).

10 Neil Smith, "There's No Such Thing as a Natural Disaster." Online at: http://understandingkatrina.ssrc.org/Smith/.

11 Louise Story and Roben Farzad, "HURRICANE KATRINA: THE COST; Insurers Estimate Damage at $9 Billion, among Costliest U.S. Storms on Record," *The New York Times.* Online at: http://www.nytimes.com/2005/08/30/us/insurers-estimate-damage-at-9-billion.html?_r=0.

12 Ibid.

13 Robert Crooks, "From the Far Side of the Urban Frontier: The Detective Fiction of Chester Himes and Walter Mosley," *College Literature* 22(3) (October, 1995), 68.

14 Ibid., 71.

15 The quotations are from Kathleen Tierney, Christine Beve, and Erica Kuligowski, "Metaphors Matter: Disaster Myths, Media Frames, and Their Consequences in Hurricane Katrina," *American Academy of Political and Social Science* 604 (March, 2006), 60–1.

16 See Amy Goodman. "Kanye West: 'Bush Doesn't Care about Black People.'" Online at: http://www.democracynow.org/2005/9/5/kanye _west_bush_doesnt_care_about.

17 Andrea Miller, Shearon Roberts, and Victoria LaPoe, *Oil and Water: Media Lessons from Hurricane Katrina and the Deepwater Horizon Disaster* (Jackson: University of Mississippi Press, 2014), 75.

18 Emma Dixon, "New Orleans' Racial Divide: An Unnatural Disaster," *Common Dreams.*

19 The quotation is from Avis Jones-Deweever, "The Forgotten Ones: Black Women in the Wake of Katrina," in Cedric Johnson (ed.), *The Neoliberal Deluge: Hurricane Katrina and the Remaking of New Orleans* (Minneapolis: University of Minnesota Press, 2011), ebook, loc. 4142.

20 Ibid., loc. 4150.

21 The quotation is from Roberta Smith, "Kara Walker Makes Contrasts in Silhouette in Her Own Met Show." Online at: http://www .nytimes.com/2006/03/24/arts/design/24walk.html?n=Top%2F Reference%2FTimes%20Topics%2FPeople%2FS%2FSmith% 2C%20Roberta&_r=0.

22 Quotations are from Anna Hartnell, "Hurricane Katrina as Visual Spectacle: *Hurricane on the Bayou* and the Reframing of American National Identity," in Tricia Cusack (ed.), *Art and Identity at the Water's Edge* (London: Ashgate, 2012), 54.

23 Ibid., 55.

24 Quotations are from Elizabeth Fussell, "Constructing New Orleans Race: A Population History of New Orleans," *The Journal of American History* 94 (December, 2007). Online at http://www .journalofamericanhistory.org/projects/katrina.Fussell.html.

25 Clyde Woods, *Development Arrested: The Blues and Plantation Power in the Mississippi Delta* (New York: Verso, 1998), 6.

26 Fussell, "Constructing New Orleans Race: A Population History of New Orleans."

27 Donald Grubbs, quoted in Woods, *Development Arrested*, 13.
28 The data are reported in Fussell, "Constructing New Orleans Race: A Population History of New Orleans."
29 Ibid.
30 See for example the collection David L. Brunsma, David Overfelt, and J. Steven Picou (eds), *The Sociology of Katrina* (Lanham, MD: Rowman & Littlefield, 2007).
31 Gilles Deleuze and Felix Guattari, *A Thousand Plateaus*, trans. Brian Massumi (Minneapolis: University of Minnesota Press, 1987), 179.
32 The quotations are from Shapiro, *Studies in Trans-Disciplinary Method: After the Aesthetic Turn* (New York: Routledge, 2012), 67.
33 Alexa Weik von Mossner, "Reframing Katrina: The Color of Disaster in Spike Lee's *When the Levees Broke*," *Environmental Communication* 5(2) (June, 2011), 151.
34 The quotations are from Adam Gussow, *It Seems Like Murder Here* (Chicago Press, 2002), 27.
35 The quotations are from Mark Wahlberg, *Documentary Time: Film and Phenomenology* (Minneapolis: University of Minnesota Press, 2008), 124.
36 The expression is in quotations because this section is edified by Mark Wahlberg's analysis of the temporalities of documentary films in his *Documentary Time*.
37 Ibid., 8.
38 The quotations in this passage are from my earlier treatment of Ellington's composition: Michael J. Shapiro, *Deforming American Political Thought* (Lexington: Kentucky University Press, 2006), 151.
39 The quotations in this passage are drawn from Maurice Peress, *Dvorak to Duke Ellington*, (New York: Oxford University Press, 2004), 182–3.
40 Shapiro, *Deforming American Political Thought*, 152.
41 The quotations are from David Schiff, *The Ellington Century* (Berkeley: University of California Press, 2012), 211.
42 See Ernest Callenbach, "When the Levees Broke: A Requiem in Four Acts," *Film Quarterly* 60(2) (Winter, 2006), 6.
43 Quoted in Vivian Sobchack, "Inscribing Ethical Space: Ten Propositions on Death, Representation, and Documentary," *Quarterly Review of Film Studies* 9(4) (1984), 283.
44 Ibid., 286.
45 Ibid., 287.
46 Quotation from Callenbach, "When the Levees Broke," 6.
47 I am quoting the words of one commentary on the documentary: Nicholas Gebhardt, "Do You Know What it Means to Miss New Orleans? Historical Metaphors and Mythical Realities in Spike Lee's 'When the Levees Broke,'" *Jazz Research Journal* 6(2) (2012). Online at: http://www.equinoxpub.com/journals/index.php/JAZZ/article/viewArticle/1752.
48 For treatments of "the black public sphere," see The Black Public Sphere Collective (ed.), *The Black Public Sphere* (Chicago: University of Chicago Press, 1995).

49 Johari Jabir, "On Conjuring Mahalia: Mahalia Jackson, New Orleans, and the Sanctified Swing," *American Quarterly* 61(3) (September, 2009), 649.
50 Benjamin displaces a simplistic continuum from past to present with episodes of shock, when the past, which "carries a temporal index ... flashes up at a moment of danger." See his "Theses on the Philosophy of History," in Hannah Arendt (ed.), *Illuminations*, trans. Harry Zone (New York: Schocken, 1968), 254–5.
51 Jabir, "On Conjuring Mahalia," 654.
52 The quoted segments are from Jacques Rancière's construal of Benjamin's messianic version of history: *Figures of History*, trans. Julie Rose (Cambridge, UK: Polity, 2014), 53.
53 Ibid., 655.
54 Herman Gray, "Recovered, Reinvented, Reimagined: Treme, Television Studies and Writing New Orleans," *Television & New Media*. Online at: http://tvn.sagepub.com/content/13/3/268.
55 Quoted in Vince Beiser, "Talking *Treme* with David Simon," *The Progressive*. Online at: https://www.progressive.org/beiser0311.html.
56 Ibid.
57 See Stanley Cavell, "The Fact of Television," *Daedalus* 11(4) (Fall, 1982), 79.
58 Ibid., 82.
59 Ibid., 89.
60 Helen A. Regis, "Blackness and the Politics of Memory in the New Orleans Second Line," *American Ethnologist* 28(4) (November, 2001), 754.
61 Quotations from ibid., 755.
62 The "listening text" expression belongs to Joy V. Fuqua, " 'In New Orleans, We Might Say It Like This ...': Authenticity, Place, and HBO's *Treme*," *Television New Media* 13(3) (2012), 237.
63 The quotations in this sentence are from Peter Osborne's astute reading of Husserl's text: *The Politics of Time: Modernity and the Avant-Garde* (London: Verso, 1995), 50.
64 Edmund Husserl, *The Phenomenology of Internal Time-Consciousness*, trans. James S. Churchill (Bloomington: Indiana University Press, 1964), 53.
65 Jacques Attali, *Noise: The Political Economy of Music*, trans. Brian Massumi (Minneapolis: University of Minnesota Press, 1985), 85.
66 Ibid., 101.
67 Ibid., 47.
68 Ibid., 101.
69 Ibid., 113.
70 See Fernand Braudel, *Afterthoughts on Material Civilization and Capitalism*, trans. Patricia Ranum (Baltimore: Johns Hopkins University Press, 1979).
71 Attali, *Noise*, 45.
72 Michael J. Shapiro, "The Moralized Economy in Hard Times," in Shapiro, *Studies in Trans-Disciplinary Method*, 40–1.

73 Joyce Oldham Appleby, *Economic Thought and Ideology in Seventeenth-Century England* (Princeton, NJ: Princeton University Press, 1978), 52.

74 Ibid., 56.

75 Igor Kopytoff, "The Cultural Biography of Things: Commoditization as Process," in Arjun Appadurai (ed.), *The Social Life of Things* (New York: Cambridge University Press, 1986), 68.

76 Attali, *Noise*, 21.

77 Kopytoff, "The Cultural Biography of Things," 68.

78 Clyde Woods, "Katrina's World: Blues, Bourbon, and the Return to the Source," *American Quarterly* 61(3) (September, 2009), 428.

79 See   http://www.theblaze.com/stories/2014/11/24/ferguson-protesters -angry-message-to-obama-democrats-this-is-obamas-katrina-and-he -aint-doing-st/.

80 Karl Mannheim, *Diagnoses of Our Time* (London: Kegan Paul, Trench, Trubner & Co, 1943), 136.

81 Benjamin, "Theses on the Philosophy of History," 254.

82 Butler, *Frames of War*, 3.

83 Ibid., 2.

84 The quotation is from Rune Saugmann Andersen, *Remediating Security: A Semiotic Framework for Analyzing How Video Speaks Security*, PhD dissertation (Department of Political Science, University of Copenhagen, 2015), 38.

85 Jacob Riis published his photographic investigation under the title *How the Other Half Lives*. For a recent edition, see *How the Other Half Lives* (New York: ReadaClassic.com, 2010).

86 The quotation is from Miriam Bader, "The Slums of New York." Online at: https://www.khanacademy.org/humanities/art-americas/ us-art-19c/us-19c-arch-sculp-photo/a/jacob-riis-how-the-other-half -lives-knee-pants-at-forty-five-cents-a-dozena-ludlow-street-sweaters -shop.

87 The concept of the metapicture belongs to W. J. T. Mitchell. See his *Picture Theory* (Chicago: University of Chicago Press, 1994).

88 Andersen, *Remediating Security*, 34.

89 See Immanuel Kant's "Analytic of the Sublime," in his *Critique of Judgment*, trans. Werner Pluhar (London: Hackett, 2011).

90 The quotations are from Eric Ishiwata, "We Are Seeing People We Didn't Know Exist: Katrina and the Neoliberal Erasure of Race," in Johnson (ed.), *The Neoliberal Deluge*, ebook, loc. 940.

91 Michael Eric Dyson, "Racial Terror, Fast and Slow." *The New York Times*. Online at: http://www.nytimes.com/2015/04/17/opinion/ racial-terror-fast-and-slow.html?_r=0.

Chapter 4   Keeping Time: The Rhythms of Work and Arts of Resistance

1 Karl Jaspers, *Reason and Existenz*, trans. William Earle (New York: Noonday, 1955), 24.

2 Ibid., 43.
3 Samuel Beckett, "Love and Lethe," in *More Pricks than Kicks* (London: Chatto and Windus, 1934), 90. It is evident that, in his reference to a "catspaw mind," Beckett was attuned to philosophical discourse, for the word "concept" in many European languages derives from the claws of a griffin – a *begriff* (German), *begrep*, (Norwegian/Danish), *begrip* (Dutch).
4 The discussion is developed in my chapter, "A Continuing Violent Cartography," in Michael Shapiro, *Studies in Trans-Disciplinary Method: After the Aesthetic Turn* (New York: Routledge, 2012), 130.
5 Cormac McCarthy, *Blood Meridian: Or the Evening Redness in the West* (New York: Vintage, 1992), 123.
6 Friedrich Nietzsche, *Thus Spake Zarathustra*, trans. A. Tille (New York: Dutton, 1960), 153.
7 McCarthy, *Blood Meridian*, 327.
8 Ibid.
9 Michel Foucault, *Discipline and Punish: The Birth of the Prison*, trans. Alan Sheridan (New York: Pantheon, 1977), 136.
10 Henri Lefebvre, *Rhythmanalysis*, trans. Stuart Elden and Gerald Moore (London: Continuum, 2004), 39–40.
11 Paul Virilio, *Speed and Politics*, trans. Mark Polizzotti (New York: Semiotext(e), 1986), 29.
12 Ibid., 30.
13 Ibid.
14 Michael Shapiro, "Toward a Politics of Now-Time: Reading *Hoop Dreams* with Kubrick's *Barry Lyndon*," in *Cinematic Political Thought* (New York: New York University Press, 1999), 28.
15 E. P. Thompson, "Work-Discipline and Industrial Capitalism," *Past & Present* 38 (December, 1967), 82.
16 Ibid., 85.
17 Ibid., 86.
18 Frantz Fanon, *The Wretched of the Earth*, trans. Constance E. Farrington (New York: Grove Press, 1966), 254–5.
19 Ibid. 254.
20 Michel Foucault, *The Order of Things* (New York: Vintage, 1994), 253.
21 Ibid., 255.
22 Ibid., 257.
23 Stefano Harney, "Hapticality in the Undercommons, or from Operations Management to Black Ops," Cumma papers # 9. Online at: http://cummastudies.files.wordpress.com/2013/08/cumma-papers-9.pdf.
24 Stephen Lemons, "Alex Rivera, Director of *Sleep Dealer*, Talks Sci-Fi, Immigration, and Robot Doctors Controlled from India," *Phoenix New Times*. Online at: http://blogs.phoenixnewtimes.com/bastard/2010/08/alex_rivera_director_of_sleep.php.
25 Michael J. Shapiro, *For Moral Ambiguity: National Culture and the Politics of the Family* (Minneapolis: University of Minnesota Press, 2001), 114.

26 Reinhart Koselleck, *Futures Past: On the Semantics of Historical Time*, trans. Keith Tribe (Cambridge, MA: MIT Press, 1985), 231.
27 Franco "Bifo" Berardi, *The Uprising: On Poetry and Finance* (Los Angeles, CA: Semiotext(e), 2012), 36.
28 Ibid., 28.
29 Ibid., 19.
30 Ibid., 36.
31 Ralph Armbruster-Sandoval, *Globalization and Cross-Border Labor Solidarity in the Americas* (New York: Routledge, 2005), 1.
32 Ibid., 6.
33 Kate Macdonald, *The Politics of Global Supply Chains* (Cambridge: UK, 2014), 25.
34 Ibid., 44.
35 Armbruster-Sandoval, *Globalization and Cross-Border Labor Solidarity in the Americas*, 6.
36 For a treatment of artistic methods that employ "aesthetic subjects," see Michael J. Shapiro, *Studies in Trans-Disciplinary Method*.
37 Quoted in "Sleep Dealer Filmmaker Alex Rivera Joins Eco-Minded Film Festival" in *Hollywood Reporter*. Online at: http://www.hollywoodreporter.com/news/sleep-dealer-filmmaker-alex-rivera-652139.
38 Vincent Amiel, *Le Corps Au Cinema: Keaton, Bresson, Cassavetes* (Paris: Presses Universitaire de France, 1998), 2 (my translation).
39 Ibid., 113.
40 Ibid., 7.
41 See "Blood & Exhaustion Behind Bargain: Toys Made in China for Wal-Mart and Dollar General-Toy," *China Labor Watch*, Online at: http://digitalcommons.ilr.cornell.edu/cgi/viewcontent.cgi?article=1908&context=globaldocs.
42 See, for example, Benjamin Powell, *Out of Poverty: Sweatshops in the Global Economy* (Cambridge, UK: Cambridge University Press, 2014).
43 Among the better academic approaches, which provide ethnographic details of the hardships of individual workers, is Pun Ngai's *Made in China: Women Factory Workers in a Global Workplace* (Durham, NC: Duke University Press, 2005).
44 See Eleanor Bird and Ian Cook (eds), *followthethings.com*. Online at: http://www.followthethings.com/santasworkshop.shtml.
45 The quotation is from William Connolly, *Neuropolitics: Thinking, Culture, Speed* (Minneapolis: University of Minnesota Press, 2002), 151.
46 The quotations are from a review of the film. Online at: http://www.pbs.org/pov/maquilapolis/film_description.php.
47 I am again quoting Amiel, *Le Corps Au Cinema*, 7.
48 Rancière develops the concept of political subjectification in many places. This one is in Jacques Rancière, *Dis-Agreement*, trans. Julie Rose (Minneapolis: University of Minnesota Press, 1999), 35.
49 Jacques Attali, *Noise: The Political Economy of Music*, trans. Bian Massumi (Minneapolis: University of Minnesota Press, 1985), 13.

50 Ibid., 92.
51 See Marek Korczynski, Emma Robertson, and Michael Pickering, *Rhythms of Labour: Music at Work in Britain* (Cambridge, UK: Cambridge University Press, 2013), 33.
52 Ibid., 144.
53 Ibid., 7.
54 Ibid., 204.
55 Ibid., 211.
56 Ibid., 208.
57 Ibid., 211.
58 Ibid., 225.
59 The quotation is from Nathaniel Mackey, "Other: From Noun to Verb," *Representations* 39 (Summer, 1992), 60.
60 The quotation is from LeRoi Jones (aka Amiri Baraka), *Blues People: Negro Music in White America* (New York: Harper, 1999), 181.
61 Mackey, "Other: From Noun to Verb," 60.
62 The quotation is mine, from Michael Shapiro, *Methods and Nations: Cultural Governance and the Indigenous Subject* (New York: Routledge, 2004), 94.
63 See Richard A. Peterson, *Creating Country Music: Fabricating Authenticity* (Chicago: University of Chicago Press, 1997), 59–60.
64 The quotations are from my chapter, "The 'Musico-Literary' Aesthetics of Attachment and Resistance," in Shapiro, *Methods and Nations*, 82.
65 Mark Franko, *The Work of Dance: Labor, Movement, and Identity in the 1930s* (Middletown, CT: Wesleyan University Press, 2002), 31.
66 Ibid.
67 Siegfried Kracauer, "Girls in Crisis" (1931) in Anton Kaes, Martin Jay, and Edward Dimendberg (eds), *The Weimar Republic Source Book* (Berkeley: University of California Press, 1994), 565 (quoted in ibid., 32).
68 Franko, *The Work of Dance*, 32.
69 Ibid., 71.
70 Ibid.
71 Ibid., 73.
72 Ibid.
73 Randy Martin, "A Precarious Dance, a Derivative Sociality," *TDR* 56(4) (Winter, 2012), 68.
74 Gilles Deleuze and Felix Guattari, *A Thousand Plateaus* (Minneapolis: University of Minnesota Press, 1987), 315.
75 The quotation is from Geoffrey Whitehall, "Musical Modulations of Political Thought," *Theory & Event* 9(3) (2006), 12.
76 The quotation is from Rick Altman, *The American Film Musical* (Bloomington: Indiana University Press, 1987), 106.
77 The quotation is from an interview with Von Trier. Online at: http:/blogs.indiewire.com/pressplay/video-essay-lars-von-trier-cinemas-dancer-in-the-dark.

78 Ibid.
79 The quotations are from "South African: Gumboot Dance," *World Arts West*. Online at: worldartswest.org/plm/guide/printablepages/gumboot.pdf. I am grateful to Sam Opondo for calling the gumboot dance to my attention.
80 Dominic Pettman, *Human Error: Species-Being and Media Machines* (Minneapolis: University of Minnesota Press, 2011), 2.
81 Bruce Robbins, "The Sweatshop Sublime." Online at http://www.columbia.edu/~bwr2001/papers/sweatshop.pdf.
82 Ibid.
83 See Immanuel Kant, *Critique of Judgment*, trans. J. H. Bernard (Amherst, NY: Prometheus Books, 2000), 88, 91.
84 The quotations are from Lyotard's succinct summary of the feeling associated with the sublime as Kant conceives it: Jean-François Lyotard, *Lessons on the Analytic of the Sublime*, trans. Elizabeth Rottenberg (Stanford, CA: Stanford University Press, 1994), 53.
85 Robbins, "The Sweatshop Sublime."
86 Ibid.
87 Ibid.
88 Kant, *Critique of Judgment*, 119.
89 Michael J. Shapiro, "The Sublime Today: Re-Partitioning the Global Sensible," in *Cinematic Geopolitics*, 97.
90 Robbins, "The Sweatshop Sublime."
91 See Kant, *Critique of Judgment*, 130.
92 Shapiro, *Cinematic Geopolitcs* 97, quoting from Jacques Rancière, "The Sublime from Lyotard to Schiller: Two Readings of Kant and Their Political Significance," *Radical Philosophy* 126 (2004), 12.
93 Robbins, "The Sweatshop Sublime."
94 Jaimey Hamilton Faris, *Uncommon Goods: Global Dimensions of the Readymade* (Chicago: Intellect, 2013), 8.
95 Ibid., 75.

Chapter 5   "Fictions of Time": Necro-Biographies

1 Grégoire Chamayou, *A Theory of the Drone*, trans. Janet Lloyd (New York: The New Press, 2015), 49.
2 The concept of a "counter-vision" is developed by David Michael Levin, "Introduction," in Levin (ed.), *Modernity and the Hegemony of Vision* (Berkeley: University of California Press, 1993), 7.
3 I do an extended analysis of Smith's story in an earlier study: *War Crimes, Atrocity, and Justice* (Cambridge, UK: Polity, 2015).
4 Zadie Smith, "The Embassy of Cambodia," *The New Yorker* (February 11 and 18, 2013), 88.
5 Ibid., 89–91.
6 Michael J. Shapiro, "Introduction" in *War Crimes: Atrocity Justice and the Archives* (Cambridge, UK: Polity, 2015).
7 Smith, "The Embassy of Cambodia," 92.
8 Ibid.

9 Imre Kertész, *Fiasco*, trans. Tim Wilkinson (Brooklyn, NY: Melville House, 2011), 45.
10 Ibid.
11 Imre Kertész, *Dossier K*, trans. Tim Wilkinson (Brooklyn, NY: Melville House, 2006), 133.
12 Smith, "The Embassy of Cambodia," 89.
13 Ibid.
14 Gilles Deleuze, *Proust and Signs* trans. Richard Howard (Minneapolis: University of Minnesota Press, 2000), 81–2.
15 The quotation is from a gloss on Deleuze's concept of the encounter by Simon O'Sullivan, *Art Encounters: Deleuze and Guattari Thought Beyond Representation* (London: Palgrave Macmillan, 2006), 1.
16 Marjorie Cohen, "Introduction: A Frightening New Way of War," in Marjorie Cohen (ed.), *Drones and Targeted Killing: Legal, Moral, and Geopolitical Issues* (Northampton, MA: Olive Branch Press, 2015), 13.
17 Michael J. Shapiro, *War Crimes, Atrocity, and Justice* (Cambridge, UK: Polity, 2015), 81.
18 Harold Garfinkel, *Studies in Ethnomethodology* (Malden MA: Polity, 1991), 16.
19 Jacques Lacan, "The Eye and the Gaze," in *The Four Fundamental Concepts of Pyscho-Analysis*, trans. Alan Sheridan (New York: Penguin, 1977), 73.
20 Ibid., 89.
21 Ibid., 103.
22 "Living Under Drones: Death, Injury, and Trauma to Civilians from US Drone Practices in Pakistan," by the International Human Rights and Conflict Resolution Clinic of the Stanford Law School and the Global Justice Clinic of the NYU Law School. Online at: http://livingunderdrones.org/.
23 Ibid.
24 See Peter Bergen, "John Brennan, Obama's Drone Warrior," *CNNOpinion*. Online at: http://www.cpm/2013/01/07/opinion/bergen-brennan-drones/.
25 See Helen M. Kinsella, *The Image Before the Weapon: A Critical History of the Distinction between Combatant and Civilian* (Ithaca, NY: Cornell University Press, 2011), 2–3.
26 See Spencer Ackerman, "CIA Drones Kill Large Groups Without Knowing Who They Are," *Wired*. Online at: http://www.wired.com/2011/11/cia-drones-marked-for-death/.
27 See "Commentary: 'Do No Harm,'" *C4ISA Journal* 4/25/2012. Online at: http://www.defensenews.com/article/20120425/C4ISR02/304250001/Commentary-8216-Do-No-Harm-8217-html.
28 Marshall Sahlins, *The Counter-Counterinsurgency Manual* (Chicago: Prickly Paradigm Press, 2009), vi.
29 Grégoire Chamayou, *Manhunts: A Philosophical History* (Princeton, NJ: Princeton University Press, 2012), 6.
30 Frank Sauer and Niklas Schörnig, "Killer Drones: The 'Silver Bullet' of Democratic Warfare?" *Security Dialogue* 43(4) (2012), 373.
31 Ibid., 370.

32 Michael J. Shapiro, *War Crimes, Atrocity, and Justice* (Cambridge, UK: Polity, 2015), 15.
33 Michel Foucault, "What is Critique?" in *The Politics of Truth*, trans. Lysa Hochroth and Catherine Porter (New York: Semiotext(e)), 47.
34 Ibid.
35 Grégoire Chamayou, *A Theory of the Drone* (New York, New Press, 2015), 17.
36 Ibid., 39.
37 Ibid., 47.
38 Paul Virilio, *A Landscape of Events*, trans. Julie Rose (Cambridge, MA: MIT Press, 2000), 43.
39 Chamayou, *A Theory of the Drone*, 49.
40 A. J. Gurevich, *Patterns of Medieval Culture* (Princeton, NJ: Princeton University Press, 1985), 294.
41 Ibid.
42 See Carlo Ginsburg, *The Cheese and the Worms: The Cosmos of a Sixteenth-Century Miller*, trans. John and Ann Tedeschi (New York: Penguin, 1982).
43 Michel Foucault, "On the Concept of the 'Dangerous Individual' in Nineteenth-Century Legal Psychiatry," *International Journal of Law and Psychiatry* 1(1) (1978): 1–18.
44 See Stephanie Clifford, "Defendants Using Biographical Videos to Show Judges Another Side at Sentencing," *New York Times*. Online at: http://www.nytimes.com/2015/05/25/nyregion/defendants-using-biographical-videos-to-show-judges-another-side-at-sentencing.html.
45 Michel Foucault, *Society Must Be Defended*, trans. David Macey (New York: Picador, 2003), 241.
46 I am quoting from my chapter, "Reading Biography," in Michael J. Shapiro, *The Politics of Representation: Writing Practices in Biography, Photography and Policy Analysis* (Madison: University of Wisconsin Press, 1988), 65–6.
47 Ibid., 72.
48 Ibid.
49 Sigmund Freud, *Leonardo Da Vinci: A Study in Psychosexuality*, trans. A. A. Brill (New York: Random House, 1947), 56.
50 Ibid.
51 Ibid.
52 Edmund Harris, *Dutch: A Memoir of Ronald Reagan* (New York: Random House, 1999).
53 Mark Maslan, "Telling to Live the Tale: Ronald Reagan, Edmund Morris, and Postmodern Nationalism," *Representations* 98(1) (Spring, 2007), 63.
54 Ibid.
55 Cathy Caruth, "Literature and the Enactment of Memory (Duras, Resnais, *Hiroshima Mon Amour*), in *Unclaimed Experience: Trauma, Narrative, and History* (Baltimore, MD: The Johns Hopkins University Press, 1996), 27.

56 Jacques Rancière, "Fictions of Time," in Grace Hellyer and Julian Murphet (eds), *Rancière and Literature* (Edinburgh: Edinburgh University Press, forthcoming, 2016).
57 Ibid.
58 Ibid.
59 Ibid.
60 Quoted in Maslan, "Telling to Live the Tale," 71.
61 Michael Rogin, *Ronald Reagan the Movie: And Other Episodes of Demonology* (Berkeley: University of California Press, 1987), 3.
62 Ibid., 11.
63 Chamayou, *A Theory of the Drone*, 49.
64 Teju Cole, "Death in the Browser Tab," *New York Times Magazine* (May 21, 2015), 20.
65 Gilles Deleuze, *Cinema 1: The Movement Image*, trans. Hugh Tomlinson and Barbara Habberjam (Minneapolis: University of Minnesota Press, 1986), 65.
66 Ibid., 14.
67 The quotation is from Erika Eicheberger, "Look at This Visualization of Drone Strike Deaths," *Mother Jones*. Online at: http://www.motherjones.com/politics/2013/03/drone-strikes-interactive-visualization-pitch. To see the site, go to: http://drones.pitchinteractive.com.
68 Wesley Grubbs is quoted in Kelsey D. Atheron, "Who are the Casualties of America's Drone Strikes?", *Popular Science* [Infographic]. Online at: http://www.popsci.com/technology/article/2013-03/casualties-drone-war-infographic.
69 Russell Banks, *Continental Drift* (New York: Ballantine, 1985), 39.
70 Richard Maxwell, "Surveillance: Work, Myth, and Policy," *Social Text* 83 (Summer, 2005), 1.
71 See http://www.nytimes.com/2015/06/09/world/middleeast/families-of-drone-strike-victims-in-yemen-file-suit-in-washington.html?_r=0.
72 See Michael J. Shapiro, "The Ethics of Encounter: Unreading, Unmapping the Imperium," in David Campbell and Michael J. Shapiro (eds), *Moral Spaces: Rethinking Ethics and World Politics* (Minneapolis: University of Minnesota Press, 1999), 57–91.
73 Ibid., 61.
74 See Joseph Conrad, "Geography and Some Explorers," in Richard Curle (ed.), *Last Essays* (London: J. M. Dent & Sons, 1926), 10–17.
75 See Rey Chow, *The Age of the World Target: Self-Referentiality in War, Theory, and Comparative Work* (Durham, NC: Duke University Press, 2006).
76 "Composition" is in quotation marks because I am here inspired by Gertrude Stein's perspective on how what is seen is a result of a composition; see her "Composition as Explanation." Online at: http://www.poetryfoundation.org/learning/essay/238702.
77 Roland Barthes, *Camera Lucida*, trans. Richard Howard (New York: Hill and Wang, 1982), 96.
78 Godard, "Hiroshima Notre Amour," 62.
79 The expression belongs to Amos Vogel, quoted in Vivian Sobchack, "Inscribing Ethical Space," in *Carnal Thoughts: Embodiment and*

Moving Image Culture (Berkeley: University of California Press, 2004), 226.

80 Ibid., 240.
81 Deleuze, *Cinema 1*, 103.
82 The "humane" gaze is part of Vivian Sobchack's inventory of the way the documentary gaze articulates and ethics: *Carnal Thoughts*, 249.
83 The quotation, which appeared in a fuller version in Don DeLillo, "American Blood: A Journey Through the Labyrinth of Dallas and JFK," *Rolling Stone*, December 8, 1983, is from my reading of his novel *Libra*: Michael J. Shapiro, "American Fictions and Popular Culture," in *Reading the Postmodern Polity: Political Theory as Textual Practice* (Minneapolis: University of Minnesota Press, 1992), 69.
84 Marco Abel, *Violent Affect: Literature, Cinema, and Critique after Representation* (Lincoln: University of Nebraska Press, 2007), 189.
85 Nasser Hussain, "The Sound of Terror: Phenomenology of a Drone Strike." Online at: http://www.bostonreview.net/world/hussain-drone -phenomenology.
86 Ibid.
87 Walter Benjamin, "The Work of Art in the Age of Mechanical Reproduction," in Hannah Arendt (ed.), *Illuminations*, trans. Harry Zohn (New York: Schocken, 1968), 238.

Afterword

1 Maclear, *Beclouded Vision: Hiroshima-Nagasaki and the Art of Witness* (Albany: State University of New York Press, 1999), 4.
2 Woods, "Katrina's World: Blues, Bourbon, and the Return to the Source," *American Quarterly* 61(3) (September, 2009), 428.
3 Immanuel Kant, *The Critique of Judgement*, trans. James Creed Meredith (Oxford, UK: 1952), 106.
4 Ibid., 99.
5 Rudolph Makkreel, "Imagination and Temporality in Kant's Theory of the Sublime," *The Journal of Aesthetics and Art Criticism* 2(3) (Spring, 1984), 306.
6 Kant, *The Critique of Judgement*, 107–8.
7 Makkreel, "Imagination and Temporality in Kant's Theory of the Sublime," 308.
8 The quotation is from Zourabichvili, *Deleuze: A Philosophy of the Event*, 143.
9 Mark Wahlberg, *Documentary Time: Film and Phenomenology* (Minneapolis: University of Minnesota Press, 2008), 8.
10 Ibid.
11 Marker, quoted in ibid.

Index

Page numbers in *italics* denote an illustration